SPIRITUAL SONGS IV:

DUSK THROUGH DAWN

"Head bowed, kneeling under the dark skies, I pray may we the humans upon Earth be safe and protected eternally from dusk through dawn."

Ann Marie Ruby

Disclaimer:

This book ("***Spiritual Songs IV: Dusk Through Dawn***") only represents the personal views of the author. In no way, does it represent or endorse any religious, philosophical, political, or scientific view. It has been written in good faith for people of all cultures and beliefs. Any resemblance to actual persons, living or dead, is purely coincidental.

Published in the United States of America, 2026.

ISBN-13: 979-8-9917416-6-8

DEDICATION

*"The Sun sets as the Moon rises
within its reflection, and reminds
all creation of the one Creator,
until dawn, carry within your souls,
hope, faith, and belief."*

Travelers traveling the lonely path of life through darkness from dusk through dawn, hold on to your faith. Know there is always a prayer which is a staircase or a bridge that will connect you the creation to your Creator as we all come from God, and we shall go back to God. In between we have the journey through life. Live in peace and spread peace. Live with one another, not against for in union we are all the creation of the one Creator.

I dedicate this book to all looking for strength, guidance, and help through their journey of life as we are all the one creation of the one Creator.

TABLE OF CONTENTS

INTRODUCTION

"The one creation
Of the one Creator
Of the one world,
We are not divided
But united.
For the Creator,
As the creation
From dusk through dawn,
We recite in union,
Spiritual Songs."

Evolution from dusk to dawn is the first miracle of the world we the creation of the one Creator witness. When dawn breaks through and dissolves the darkness, the world rejuvenates with hope. The first glimpse of dawn is highly auspicious for new beginnings, strengthening our beliefs, and awakening ourselves as we have crossed over the darkness and have landed upon the light. The miracle becomes a reality as we walk out of the darkness with the first kiss of dawn.

My lips start to pray as I greet my mornings with the knowledge that darkness lost to the first light of dawn. I watched the sunset and darkness cover the world, where I the human remained hopeless. Yet then, I again watched the Sun come back up and remove the darkness, not through the work of any human but by the grace of our Creator, the Omnipotent. So, in the morning before I start to plan my day, I awaken myself with faith, hope, and belief that whatever takes place, my God, the Creator is there.

The morning sets a precedent for how our days will be or how we would like our days to be. Every morning, we the humans greet the day with faith, hope, and belief. As the dark night disappears, I realize not everything is lost for we the humans are all connected to the Creator through our faith. We welcome dawn differently at different times and places, yet we acknowledge our Creator and His blessed creations of day, night, the Earth, the stars, and the complete celestial bodies. The miracle of daybreak is the only testimony I need for my faith and belief in my God, my Creator. I know with faith, hope, and belief, darkness will evaporate.

My Creator, I know a lot of humans are suffering tonight. Some are in pain, some need financial assistance, some need a helping hand, and so much more I cannot begin and finish with words. Yet the obstacles seem to never end, and the tears of my God's creation seem to never stop falling. If tonight you feel hopeless, I want to reassure you to never lose hope, never lose faith, and never give up. Tonight is dark and it might get even darker, but dawn is around the corner. Your life's troubles will be over as you cross over the dark times into the first glimpse of dawn in your life.

In the interim period, I want you all to hold on to this book and read whichever prayer you open. Feel the love for your Creator, and know He loves you and is there with you even if you cannot see Him. Feel Him through these prayers I call songs. Let these spiritual songs written by a human for all humans, touch your inner soul. Let them be there for you during the darkest time of your life. Hold on to them, get on the ladder of hope, and know you will soon land upon dawn.

Each morning, dawn breaks open and greets us with a smile. Whatever frightful events the dark night had brought seem less scary at dawn. As a child, I was scared that something was hiding under my bed. At times, I felt something scary touched my feet. I would try to turn the lights on but knew I had to overcome my fear by just sleeping out the night because dawn would soon break through. Then, as a grown up, I shed all my hidden tears I did not want any witnesses to in the middle of the night. When dawn awakened me, I felt lighter as if a burden had been lifted even though nothing had changed. In my heart, I realized it was another day.

Every morning, I feel like the magical Sun and his glory evaporate all the fears of the dark night. So, this prayer book in my *Spiritual Songs* collection is called *Dusk Through Dawn*, as each new dawn blesses us by spreading joy around the universe. It is a blessing our Creator has blessed upon us when He created the brightest star we can see, the Sun, to be with us and guide us. Rejuvenate your faith and believe in the Creator, whatever you choose to call Him. He calls you His creation as He is the one Creator of all His creation. Open this blessed book and welcome the warmth and the power of dawn's blessings in your own life.

I, a creation of my Creator, walked through hardships and stopped on the bridge of obstacles, praying on my knees. When I finally reached the calm twilight hours, after crossing all the obstacles, I penned for you and me, my book of hope with 101 prayers for 101 nights. Today, I have as my personal gift for all creation of the one Creator of the one world, my book of songs I call *Spiritual Songs IV: Dusk Through Dawn*, to be there for you during your time of need.

PRAYERS:

Dusk Through Dawn

ARRIVAL OF DAWN

Darkness exists everywhere.
Even where I place
My trust,
It is broken
As the temptations
Of the dark night's
Sinful predators
Seem sweet and innocent.
Oh my God,
As I the innocent
Am discarded and ignored
By the sinful
And mighty crowd,
Protect me
From the wrong.
Oh my God,
The grounds above Earth
Are muddy.
The oceans
Are murky
As the water rises from the oceans
And pours itself

All around the Earth
After washing
The sins of the sinners.
How do I open the eyes of all
Who have eyes,
Yet do not see?
Who have ears,
Yet refuse to hear?
Who know the difference
Between good and bad,
Yet refuse to acknowledge
The difference?
Where the temptations
Are mightier
Than the righteous,
How do I make
A difference,
My God, my Creator?
For tonight,
As I travel through
This dark frightful
Night's path,
I sturdy myself.
I take control of

My earthly vehicle.
I know it is
Not who I can change,
But me who must stand my grounds
And be the pious.
I must not fall prey
To the temptations of life,
For my job is
To avoid all temptations
And the deadly sins.
My God, my Creator,
I ask You for guidance.
I seek You for knowledge.
I knock on Your door of mercy
To be safe and pious,
To have the virtues
You bless the pious with,
And to be able to say
No
To all that is wrong and sinful.
Oh my God,
May I be blessed with
The knowledge of
The wrong and the right.

Oh my God,
May I not fall prey to anything
That is forbidden.
Oh my God,
As I walk through
The dark and lonely path,
May You,
My God,
Walk with me.
May You hold my hands
And never let go
Even throughout
The darkest nights.
Oh my God,
I ask,
I seek,
And I knock
On Your door
To never let me go
And to guide me through
The darkest part of my life
To the blessed
ARRIVAL OF DAWN.

So Be It

AS DAWN RISES

As dusk evolves into darkness,
With love,
I kneel with grace,
Place my hands together
With all my faith,
And look up
As I pray to the Creator,
The Omnipotent.
Oh my God,
The darkness becomes petrifying
As I encounter
Men and women
Walking into
Different houses of worship.
They look at me
And they tell me
To pray like them,
Yet, I ask You,
My God,
My Creator,
Who do I pray like?
Which house of worship

Do I enter?
I find it hurtful
Not the way they treat me,
But each other,
As everyone declares
Their way,
Their word,
And their house
Are the complete truth.
Everyone declares
The ones
Who are different,
And who pray differently
As fallacious.
Oh my God,
I, Your creation,
Am not afraid of You,
Yet why am I afraid
Of Your creation?
I fear their comments.
I fear their looks.
I fear their actions.
Yet as I walk by
The houses of worship,

I realize all are
Just praying
And just trying to do
What they think is right
To be upon the right path.
I smile and say to all,
I believe in
The God,
The Omnipotent.
I believe in His Path.
I believe in life
And in death.
I believe all are His creation
As I am too His creation.
I believe
All different paths
Will take us to the house of
The Omnipotent.
I believe darkness will evaporate,
As I know
With all my faith,
Truth comes to light
AS DAWN RISES.

So Be It

AS DAWN'S BLESSINGS

Oh my God,
Confusion surrounds me,
Yet I know You have
The solution.
I find myself overburdened
With questions,
Yet I know the answers
Lay with only You.
Oh my God,
The Omnipotent,
The Omnipresent,
I pray to You
For the solutions.
I pray to You for the answers.
I pray to You for guidance.
I am in distress,
Which path should I take?
Where do I go?
How do I go
When I neither
Have the direction
Nor the answers

To my questions?
Oh my God,
What should I do?
Afraid and lost,
Unsettled and angry
At my own self,
I do not know which path
To take.
My God, my Creator,
The All-Knowledgeable,
The All-Knowing,
The Forgiver,
The Giver of sustenance,
I pray to You.
For when and where we,
Your creation,
Have no one,
We have You.
You are our Protector.
You are our Guide.
You are our only hope.
When and where
There is nothing,
Or no one,

Yet one has faith,
Then and there,
My God, my Creator,
You appear.
You gift the destitute.
You direct the lost
And stranded.
You embrace the creation
Who never lost faith,
Who never lost hope,
And who never lost their path
Through the journey of life.
So today,
As I try to walk forward,
Toward the right path,
As I try to make
The right decision,
As I try to enter
Your chosen place,
Your chosen home,
And Your chosen work,
The ones You have blessed,
I ask,
Seek,

And knock,
On Your doors
Through my blessed prayers
To take me to the place, the home, and the work
You have chosen.
Oh my God,
For even when all is lost,
My lips still recite
Your name
Through my sacred prayers.
As I close my eyes
To see You,
I open my ears to listen to
The words
You may have sent.
I open my inner heart
For answers
You may have sent.
Oh my God,
Today,
As I walk through
The darkest part
Of my journey,
I pray

With all my faith
And belief
To only You.
For I know all can leave me,
All can forget me,
Yet my God,
My Creator,
Will always answer my prayers.
I will never stop praying
For I shall worship You,
My God, my Creator,
All throughout the night
And throughout the day.
Even when my journey
Seems never ending,
And the day
Finds no solutions,
I shall continue to pray
As I believe
My God shall provide me
With answers through
His blessings
AS DAWN'S BLESSINGS.

So Be It

ASPIRATION OF DAWN

Oh my God, my Creator,
I stand upon a dark
And frightful night
Where financial burdens
Suffocate me,
Where physical pain
Burdens me,
Where a life without love or purpose
Drifts me toward the wrong path.
Oh my God, my Creator,
Tonight,
I raise my hands
In prayer to You
As I know where and when
Nothing is found,
Nothing is answered,
Everything seems lost,
A prayer call to You
Is the only hope.
A prayer call to You
Is my complete faith
As that is when

I awaken and know
To never lose faith
And to never lose hope.
A prayer call is the only thing
I, Your creation,
Was born with.
That is the only thing
I shall carry with me eternally.
Where hope thrives,
Everything is found.
Where faith lives,
Nothing is lost.
Throughout the dark, cold, and frightening night,
I shall keep
My lantern of hope
And my glowing faith
Lit for myself
And all the travelers of life
If they too are lost and stranded
Upon the burdens of life.
With my lantern of hope
And my glowing faith,
I can find myself
And guide myself

Out of my misery,
And be a guide
For all those
Who find themselves
Upon the same lost path in life.
Oh my God, my Creator,
As I carry my lantern of hope,
And my glowing faith with me,
I teach all how to make
Their own lanterns of hope
And glowing faith.
I know You,
Oh my God, my Creator,
Have answered my prayers
Through Your biggest,
Brightest candle which
Even after the darkest periods
Of the night,
Stays firm and smiles.
With hope and faith,
He says everything shall be
Just all right.
My God, my Creator,
You have for me,

Your beloved creation,
With love and with care,
Created the brightest star to appear
After the darkest times of my life,
Reassuring me
To never lose faith
And to never go astray.
After all dark times,
I find myself filled
With complete faith and hope.
The biggest and brightest star,
Fighting its own battles
Against the dark times,
Reappears in front of me,
Reassuring me
To never give up on faith
And to never give up on hope
As that is my God's message for me.
He sends with
A bright smiling face
His biggest star
As my
ASPIRATION OF DAWN.

So Be It

AT THE BREAK OF DAWN

Oh my God,
My Creator,
The Earth bids farewell
To the day
As the Sun sets
Within Your vast skies.
Oh my God,
The Omnipotent,
I watch
The golden embers set
In the vast faraway ocean
As I pray for myself
And all Your creation.
May we,
Your creation,
Not be left or forgotten
In the dark.
Oh my God,
Bless us.
Show us the way
As we kneel,
Bow our heads,

Raise our hands,
And pray.
Oh my God,
I watch Your shining stars
Start to blink
In the dark night's skies
As Your bright
Shining Moon smiles
And shows
All the lost and stranded
Their way.
Oh my God,
I pray
May all darkness,
All fear,
And all worries
Fade away as we pray
With hope,
With faith,
And with devotion
From the hours of
Sunset to sunrise
AT THE BREAK OF DAWN.

So Be It

AT THE FIRST ARRIVAL OF DAWN

Oh my God,
The Omnipotent,
Your Sun sets
As Your creation
Are frightened,
Are scared,
And are lost
In the dark night's lost path.
Oh my God,
I ask You,
Why do You
Send darkness?
Oh my God,
Why does life get hard?
Oh my God,
Why in this tough life,
Do I, Your blessed creation,
Feel lost?
As I walk through
The dark night's lost path,
Everything seems impossible.
All that I seek

Seem so far away.
I call upon my faith
To find hope,
So I can go on
Even through the burdens of life.
Oh my God,
May my feet
Not stop or fall or trip
On the dark path.
Oh my God,
My whole being
Freezes in fear.
What is in front of me is unknown
As I left behind me
Only troubles of life.
Oh my God,
Show me the path.
Give me hope.
Let my faith carry me
Through the hurdles of life.
As I stand at the crossroad
Of the dark night,
I know the Sun
Has set for the day.

He left me
Stranded in the dark.
As I kneel,
As I pray,
And as I spread my tears
Across the dark night's path,
I watch the glittering drops
Of my tears shine.
They dance and their reflections
Become the stars
In the dark night,
Guiding all who will
Be on the same path.
My prayer,
My message to all humans
Who follow,
Is to not give up on faith.
Hold on to hope
As my God, my Creator,
Has promised,
After the dark night,
Upon our path,
The glorious morning will return.
As the Sun sets each night,

He promises
To be back at dawn.
With faith and hope,
All the troubles will end.
My God, my Creator,
Promises
All obstacles will end,
Like the darkness
Always fades.
All the wishes
Made under
The dark skies,
Keeping the stars
As witnesses,
Will be answered.
Prayers said
Are always answered.
The glorious Sun
Created by the Creator
Never left
As the Omnipotent promises
The Sun shall appear
AT THE FIRST ARRIVAL OF DAWN.

So Be It

BE HEALED AT DAWN

My God,
The Healer,
The Remover
Of obstacles,
The Giver
Of everything,
And the Taker
Of everything,
Your devoted human,
Your blessed creation,
This morning,
Is in physical pain.
The body
Feels tired
Even though
The devoted mind and soul
Are still devoted
In worshipping
Only You.
I ask You,
My God,
The Remover

Of all illnesses,
The miraculous Healer,
The one and only God,
My Creator,
Bless this body
You have created.
Remove all
Physical obstacles
From
This physical body tonight
For You are
The Healer
Who within
Your breath,
Can take out
All physical illnesses,
As You,
My God,
Say to me,
Your creation,
Be healed!
Be healed!
BE HEALED AT DAWN.

So Be It

BEFORE DAWN BREAKS OPEN

My God, my Creator,
You are the Giver,
The Sustainer,
The One
Who knows everything
As my God,
You are the All-Knowing.
My God,
You created the Sun
To break through at dawn,
To shine light
Upon the Earth,
Yet why is it still hard
To overcome the emotional
And the physical pain
This world bestows upon me?
My God,
The All-Knowing,
I pray before dawn
To wipe away
All my emotional
And physical pain,

And to remove
All the hurdles
That have blocked my path,
That have made me destined
To the destination
I fear.
I pray
Each and every day
For a miracle to be bestowed
Upon me.
Like the miraculous
Sun glowing
Behind the dark skies,
Evaporating the darkness
From the Earth,
Bless me.
Bestow upon my destiny,
Blessings,
Guidance,
Sustenance,
Love,
Peace,
And joy,
So I, Your creation,

Can awaken at dawn
As Your Sun blesses my home
And wipes away all the darkness,
All the physical and emotional distress,
And sufferings.
My God,
The Merciful,
The All-Knowing,
Tonight,
As I raise my hands,
I pray
Through Your blessed Sun,
Erase the darkness
And allow the light in my life.
With Your blessings
And this devoted creation's
Asking,
Seeking,
And knocking
Upon Your mercy,
Oh my God,
Accept and answer this predawn prayer
BEFORE DAWN BREAKS OPEN.

So Be It

BENEDICTION OF DAWN

Oh my God,
My Creator,
The Most Powerful,
The Most Giving,
The Most Loving,
The Forgiver,
The Punisher,
I ask You to help me,
Guide me,
And protect me
Through the journey
Of my life,
Where I am
Confronted with obstacles,
Where I must live
And be within temptation.
Here I have
No teacher
Who can hold my hands.
I have no guide
Who can be there with me.
I am a lonely traveler,

Lost and stranded
Within the cold
Freezing ocean of life.
If one can float,
Or knows how to
Swim within
The murky waters,
Then, one can survive.
Yes, my God,
With Your given guidance,
Your given commandments,
I do float
And I do swim
In the murky waters.
As I swim in difficulties,
I remember
At all times,
My God is there.
I float with ease
As I recall
My God's words.
I remain clean and sober
Even within
The murky waters of life.

I pray to You
Throughout my troubles
And throughout my contentment.
I keep my God's verses
On my lips.
For even when
I hear not
Your words
And I see not
Your physical presence,
I know my God is there.
Tonight,
As the darkness covers my path,
I need financial support.
I need a safe and secure home
Away from all the dangerous humans
Who are even more frightful
Than beasts.
I need a supporting hand
To hold on to me.
I know my God
Will not remain silent.
I will ask,
I will seek,

And I will knock upon
All the doors of
Heavens above,
And keep praying.
I believe
This journey
Through the dark
And frightful night
Is my God's lesson,
My God's teaching.
Through all the obstacles,
I have not lost my faith.
I have not lost my hope.
I have not lost my belief
That my God
Will answer my prayers.
As this horrific night ends,
The biggest
Star arrives smiling,
And removes
All my obstacles
With the
BENEDICTION OF DAWN.

So Be It

BENISONS OF DAWN

My God,
The Giver of all life,
The Taker of all life,
I pray only to You
For this life
Is Your gift.
The journey through my life
Is my test.
I only ask You, my God,
To guide me
Through the obstacles
Of my life
As they are my burdens.
I knock on
Your door of forgiveness
To remove them
As You my God
Are the one and only
Remover of all obstacles.
Oh my God,
I seek the right path,
The right job,

The right house,
The right way
To get upon the right path,
The path You have lit
During the dark
And stormy nights
With candles above the skies
Which never fade,
Nor do they go astray.
They are there
Throughout the
Cyclones of life
To guide us through
The most difficult periods
Of our lives.
I pray to You, my God,
May all the storms
In my life now
Be removed.
May I, my God,
Now have only
Blessings poured upon me.
May the path I travel upon
Be blessed,

And the things I touch
And have in my life,
Be blessed.
May I not be drenched
Within pouring showers of sufferings,
But my God,
May I be blessed
With Your love,
Your guidance,
And Your mercy.
May there be
Plenty of glowing lights
As Your brightest star
Appears happily
While I recite my prayers
From dusk to dawn.
I know the losses in my life
Will fade away,
Like the dark nights
Too fade away at dawn.
Today,
I know I finally will have the
BENISONS OF DAWN.

So Be It

BLESSED MESSAGE OF DAWN

The darkest night approaches
When fear fades away
As a beloved member
Stops breathing.
As seen,
As known,
As told,
This is a journey
Everyone must cross
As everyone must return
To the God, the Creator.
We mourn,
Yet we remember.
We will never forget
The memories created
Throughout the time
We spent together.
Oh my God, my Creator,
When a human
Returns home to You
We pray at the places of worship
For forgiveness.

Yet when
A furry boy
Or a furry girl
Goes back to be with You,
We mourn alone
As not everyone
Accepts them
Into their homes of worship.
My God, my Creator,
I pray tonight
For them
To be accepted by You.
May they be loved by all
As You created them.
Oh my God,
I know there are
On this Earth,
Monstrous humans,
Who do not belong
In the society.
There are beasts
Who belong in cages,
Yet not our furry babies,
As they are innocent.

They love their human family members
All their entire living life.
My God, my Creator,
May we the family members
Left behind,
Find joy,
Find happiness,
And find comfort in knowing
They loved us
All their lives,
And it is for us now
To remember them all our lives,
Not to cry,
Not to be upset,
And not to be depressed
As they taught us
To be happy.
So, I will from this night forward,
Always remember all furry friends,
And let them be welcomed in
My home and my prayers.
I shall connect them to You
As I am Your blessed creation
Who knows they too

Are Your beloved creation,
Not welcomed
In all houses on Earth,
But welcomed in
Your house in Heaven.
As I see dawn break through,
I recite this prayer in their honor
And in their memories.
As I see the biggest star
Rise upon the dawn's skies,
I say all creation
Are God's blessings
On Earth and in Heaven.
Today, as I see the
First sight of dawn,
I pray in peace knowing
Our furry friends
Are smiling as they
Are enjoying their welcome back gifts
From God
As we smile, pray,
And recite the
BLESSED MESSAGE OF DAWN.

So Be It

BLESSED PRAYERS BEFORE DAWN

On this blessed evening,
As I await
The miraculous dawn,
After the
Restlessness and tearful worries,
I am blessed to realize,
Hope never left
My inner mind,
My body,
Or my soul.
All the obstacles,
Of this world,
All the troubles
Life gave me,
Are all being defeated
Through my hope,
My faith,
And my blessed prayers.
My Lord,
My Creator,
I send my prayers
To You

Through my pen and paper
As I write my prayers
And I manifest
My positive thoughts
To become my reality.
As positive manifesting
Is my way
Of praying to You,
My Lord,
My Creator,
Answer my prayer calls.
The dark night's obstacles
Are nothing compared to
My heartfelt prayers
Which glow
Throughout the
Dark nights.
This ever-glowing
Lantern of prayers
Shall evaporate
All obstacles
Through my
BLESSED PRAYERS BEFORE DAWN.

So Be It

BLESSINGS OF DAWN

Oh my God,
The Omnipotent,
The Omnipresent,
The Omniscient,
Show me the path.
Show me the way.
Show me the light.
I, Your creation,
Seek,
Knock,
And ask for the right path
And the right direction
To the brightest star.
Your brightest star
Can redirect me
Onto the path
Where I must be,
Where I will gather
Your blessings,
Your mercy,
And Your forgiveness.
From there,

My journey will take me
To the point of my life,
My God,
You asked me to find,
To be,
And to live within
For my protection,
For my safety,
And for Your blessings.
All the answers my mind,
My body,
And my soul seek lie there.
Without any other means,
I pray,
I pray,
And I pray
As I know my prayers
Are my beacons of hope
As through my prayers,
After the darkness of my life,
I find myself watching
The
BLESSINGS OF DAWN.

So Be It

BREAD AT DAWN

The dark night overshadows
All the gifts
Of the daylight hours.
Yet even during the dark hours,
I pray to my God,
The Omnipotent.
As I see the twinkling stars
Above the Heavenly skies
Glow above Earth,
I know my God never left.
As the Moon shines upon
The path for us,
The stranded passengers of the night,
I know hope
Glances back at me
As my eyes witness
This miraculous exchange
Of a human and the stars
Above the Heavenly skies.
It is then I know
My God is there.
For now,

I pray for dawn.
As the night gets darker,
I know dawn is around the corner.
At the first break of dawn,
I shall bake my bread.
I gather sweet butter
And warm sweet milk,
As I ready myself
To share what I have
With all those who have none.
I shall,
As dawn breaks open,
Gather what I have
And not ponder
On what I do not have.
I shall give thanks
For my bread,
My butter,
And for my milk.
I shall share and be thankful
For my family, my friends,
And my neighbors
From all different races, religions, and countries.
I shall send out

My message of gratitude
To my God,
The Creator of this Earth,
Of the Heavens above,
And of all creations.
At the first sight of dawn,
I shall remind
Myself and all others
To give grace
And be grateful
For what we have,
And not be gauche
Or ungrateful
For what we do not have.
Oh my God,
The Creator,
With complete faith,
Complete belief,
And not quitting
But trying again and again,
I shall achieve
And be at the destination
I am to be,
And not destined to be destitute

Or on the wrong path.
So, my God,
As dawn approaches me,
I, Your creation,
Raise my hands
And pray for myself
And all others
To never give up
And never lose faith,
As all prayers recited with
Complete faith,
Complete belief,
And complete confidence
Will be answered
If only we pray
With hope and faith.
So, this dawn,
My God,
I pray and I give
My morning grace
As I break and share
My
BREAD AT DAWN.

So Be It

BREAKING RAYS OF DAWN

My God, my Creator,
As dusk appears
On Earth,
Darkness takes over
The night's skies.
I, Your devoted creation,
Remember
Not to be scared,
And not to lose hope,
Or my faith,
As my God is there.
I thank You,
My God, my Creator,
For providing me
Hope,
For giving me
My faith,
And for lighting
The Earth
With the shining
Of the glorious Moon.
I thank You,

My God,
For lighting my path
With the twinkling stars
That never fade,
As I keep my hope
And my faith
Packed within
My inner mind,
Body,
And soul.
As I walk alone
Through the dark times
Of my life,
My hope and faith
Stay steadfast
As I know
My God, my Creator,
Is there.
My God,
I pray throughout
My life on Earth
And beyond,
May I,
Your devoted creation,

Never lose hope
Or my faith.
May my love
For You
And Your love
For me
Keep me steadfast.
I know
After the darkest times,
I will be greeted with
The brightest
And the biggest star
Breaking open the
Blocked doors,
Removing the darkness
From my life.
As I shall never lose my hope
Or my faith,
I shall find myself
Greeting and thanking
My God, my Creator,
For the
BREAKING RAYS OF DAWN.

So Be It

BRIGHTEST STAR AT DAWN

Stars
Upon the dark night's skies
Are glowing
And blinking
As they are praying.
The lanternfish under the ocean
Are glowing as they too join
In the night's prayers.
The fireflies have come out
As they fly glowing.
Their wings join
The blinking night stars
In the same prayer.
I, Your devoted creation, too
Have come out
With a lantern in my hand
As I join all Your creations
In the same prayer.
Tonight,
We pray to see
The miracles of our Creator,
The Omnipotent,

And we wait for
Our Creator's blessings
To be poured upon all of us,
The creations of the one Creator.
We light the path of all believers
Through faith,
All night long.
Through our combined prayers,
We witness a miracle
Finally appears,
As our Creator, our God,
Smiles and sends
His biggest blessing,
The Sun to appear,
Breaking
Open the dark night's skies,
And taking
The world out of darkness.
We, all in union,
See our prayer request
Has been answered,
As we see the
BRIGHTEST STAR AT DAWN.

So Be It

CELEBRATE LIFE FROM DAWN

Oh my God,
As the Sun sets
And the stars
All hide behind
The darkness,
I watch the sinners
And the wrong
Take liberty as
Your creation
Get lost
And ask for help.
Oh my God,
I ask,
I seek,
And I knock
Upon all doors
To awaken humanity,
To awaken all with faith,
To awaken all with candles of hope,
And not to go astray,
To hide within the darkness,
Or fall prey to the prowlers

And become the predators
Of the night.
My God,
The Omnipotent,
Has given all
A path,
A direction,
And a guide
To follow.
Oh my God,
Tonight,
I pray for the
Repented
And the redeemed sinners.
I pray for the pious
To not forget
My God,
The Omnipotent,
Has created all to follow
And not go astray
As we all have
A reason to
CELEBRATE LIFE FROM DAWN.

So Be It

DARKNESS EVAPORATES FROM DAWN

Oh my God,
The Omnipotent,
As the skies of dawn spread
Glowing amber light
Across the Earth,
I remind myself,
Before I open my eyes,
To pray.
Oh my God,
The Omnipotent,
Guide me through all obstacles,
Through all miseries,
Through all challenges,
And through all sufferings
This day brings upon me.
Oh my God,
The Omnipotent,
As dusk spreads
Golden embers
Across the Earth's skies,
I remind myself
Not to close my eyes

Until I pray.
Oh my God,
The Omnipotent,
Through the darkness,
May I not get lost
Within the challenges or the barriers,
Whether they are philosophical,
Psychological,
Or spiritual.
Oh my God,
The Omnipotent,
May I,
Even in this darkness,
Have Your help
To address these obstacles,
And may they be removed
Through my faith, hope, and belief.
All prayers
Are answered
By my God
The Omnipotent,
As
DARKNESS EVAPORATES FROM DAWN.

So Be It

DARKNESS TO DAWN

I pray to my God
My Creator,
The Omnipotent,
The Omnipresent,
The Omniscient,
On this very cloudy, rainy, and thunderous day,
Hold me and protect me
From all dangers of life.
Give me shelter
Under Your canopy of protection.
Let all dangers and all obstacles
Fade away
As You wipe away
The darkness
And let there be light.
You lift me
With Your blessed hands
And take me away for my safety
From all of life's obstacles and hurdles,
As You change
DARKNESS TO DAWN.

So Be It

DAWN BECOMES A NEW DAY

On this blessed day,
My God, my Creator,
The Omnipotent,
I sit on my knees
And I pray to never get lost
Or forget
Your blessings
And go astray.
The journey,
Through this life
Only lasts for a day,
Where nothing is found,
Where nothing is left,
And where nothing is
Without Your say.
So, I remember to pray
As I say,
May I never go astray
As the dark night's darkness fades
And
DAWN BECOMES A NEW DAY.

So Be It

DAWN BREAKS THROUGH

As dawn comes within sight,
I know soon everything
Will be all right.
The fearful nights,
The worrisome times,
And the painful hours
Will soon disappear.
Within the night's
Danger-filled darkness,
I wait through
The hurdles of my life.
Even through
The darkest part of my life,
I never lose hope,
Nor do I
Give up on faith
As I give
My God, the Omnipotent,
A phone call
Through my prayers.
My communication is peaceful.
This communication

Between a creation
And the Creator
Is not asking,
Is not seeking,
And is not knocking for material things,
But for a solution.
I know my God listens
To my prayer calls.
These prayer calls
Keep me safe.
They provide for me.
They guard me.
My prayer calls never end,
Nor do they give up
As they have within them,
Hope,
As they are made through
Faith.
They hold on to me,
As I never give up
On my prayer calls.
These prayer calls
Are communications
Between a creation

And the Creator.
I ask my Creator
On this frightful night
To not hang up on
Or disconnect my prayer calls.
Through these blessed and powerful
Graceful words,
I know I am saved.
I am provided for.
I will take the right path.
I will avoid the cursed path,
And when traveling
Through the obstacles,
I will be carried by
My God, my Creator.
Tonight,
I again raise my hands
And I bow my head
As I ask,
Seek,
And knock upon the doors
Of the Omnipotent
For guidance.
May I have a way

To earn the sustenance.
May I have a way
To buy my house
And keep it safe for my family
From the dangers
That loom around in the dark.
May I have a way to keep my loved ones
Safe and protected.
May I have the way
And may I find the solutions
As the troubles knock
Upon my doors.
May I, Your devoted creation,
Through my will and efforts,
Find the solutions
To all my problems.
I believe in miracles
Through effort, trial, and errors,
Yet I believe in
My God,
His miracles,
And His solutions
As I believe my prayer calls,
Which are between

A creation and the Creator,
Never go unheard
As prayer calls
Are the only connection
We have with
Our Creator, the Omnipotent.
So tonight,
I pray for a miracle.
I pray for a blessing.
I pray for the darkness
To disappear,
And I pray for
My God's intercession
For the dark times
To be over.
May all
The innocent prayer calls
Be answered
And the troubles be over
As all darkness evaporates
Each night,
And after a long night,
DAWN BREAKS THROUGH.

So Be It

DAWN COMES AFTER DUSK

Oh my God,
My Creator,
As the Sun sets
And places me into dusk,
And then
Into darkness,
I do not panic.
I do not fall.
I do not ever
Lose my footings
As I hold on to
My never wilting faith,
While lighting
My glowing lanterns of hope.
With my unwavering faith,
I shall only worship You.
Never shall I give up on You,
Even when this darkness
Keeps telling me,
You, my God,
Have forgotten me.
I shall carry

My lantern of hope
To light my path,
And for all who get
Lost on the same path
After me
Or with me.
Oh my God,
I shall cross the oceans.
I shall climb the mountains.
I shall walk across the Earth
As I know,
I have my faith with me
As my guiding support.
I know in the ocean,
You, my God, shall come
With Your Ark.
I believe You will come
Down from the mountain
And carry me up.
I believe You,
My God,
Shall walk with me
As I try to travel
Across the Earth

Only for You
And with You invisibly
As my visible support.
Never shall I lose hope.
Never shall my faith wilt
As I have the blessings
And guidance
Of my faith,
And my unwavering belief
With me as my guide.
My God, the Omnipotent,
I pray You
Carry me across
Dusk to the dark night,
And then carry me
Safely to dawn.
I have with me
My unwavering faith,
And my prayers
Which I shall recite
From dusk to dawn,
As I know
DAWN COMES AFTER DUSK.

So Be It

DAWN COMES AGAIN

My God,
My Creator,
Tonight,
I pray to You
As I am the lost traveler.
I know the path is there.
I know the journey
Must be made.
Yet, my God,
I, Your creation,
Am confused.
I am worried.
I am stressed
As what, where, and how
Should I proceed?
I need mercy,
Guidance,
And blessings.
I ask,
I seek,
And I knock
Upon Your doors for help.

Oh my God,
Make a miracle be
Like the miraculous light
Of Your glorious Sun.
Hold on to me,
And take me
To the place I belong,
Where I must be,
As You can
Part the sea.
You can take me
To the mountain top,
Or with Your blessed hands,
You can bring the mountain
To me
Like a clay pot,
If so You wish.
With complete
Faith and hope,
I believe with
This blessed prayer,
I will be saved.
I will be guided.
I will be provided for

As with this miraculous prayer
That is recited
From my inner soul
To You,
My God,
There will be a bridge
Created for me
To walk upon safely
To my destination.
I the lost traveler
Will find my
Way back home.
I will be
The traveler,
Not the lost.
My prayers
Will find You,
My God,
My Creator.
I know
My prayers shall then be
Answered as
DAWN COMES AGAIN.

So Be It

DAWN GLOWS

Oh my God,
The Omnipotent,
As the light burns out
Within Your Earth,
Your skies turn dark.
Oh my God,
It is then,
We, Your creation,
Face darkness.
Guide us,
Bless us,
And protect us
Through the dark nights.
Oh my God,
Glow some
Miraculous stars upon us,
Which can guide
Us, Your creation,
Through all obstacles,
All hindrances,
And all difficulties,
Of this life.

Oh my God,
Hear my prayers
As I raise my hands,
Bow my head,
And kneel on my knees
For help.
Oh my God,
Accept my prayers.
Oh my God,
Show me mercy.
Oh my God,
Bless my path.
Oh my God,
Hold my hands.
Oh my God,
Carry me as the lights diminish
And darkness takes over.
I pray to You,
For I know
You, my God,
Can carry me to dawn
As after the light burns out,
DAWN GLOWS.

So Be It

DAWN SHALL RISE

My God, my Creator,
May I emerge as myself
Against the currents
Of the acceptable
And the unacceptable
By today's standards
Which my God,
Will be at the cost
Of upsetting all around me.
My ways,
My path,
And my words
Are set within Your commandments
Which avoid all the forbidden sins,
As they are
My standard of life,
Sealed, signed, and delivered
By You,
My God, my Creator.
Forgive me as on this path,
I travel,
Yet I do not condemn the others

Who do not meet
My ways of life.
I do not judge anyone
As I know it is not
For me to do.
I accept our differences
As different paths,
Different ways,
And different choices
We the travelers of life
Chose as our own choices.
All judge me
And criticize me for not
Accepting their ways.
I take the criticism,
Like becoming
The stone that weeps,
The stone that cries,
And the stone that feels,
But never shows
Feelings or judgments.
I know my God, my Creator,
Is the only Judge
We, the creation,

Shall all meet as
We travel through
The journey of life.
As we travel
Through this path,
I pray may my path
Be blessed with
Your guiding stars at night.
May I not lose hope,
Or go astray
During the dark night,
But be positive
And be filled with hope.
I know with the first sign of light,
After the hard journey
Through the darkness,
Fighting all my hurdles
And all my obstacles,
I shall always recite
Glory be to my Lord
As announcing
The end of all my troubles,
DAWN SHALL RISE.

So Be It

DAWN SMILES UPON US

My God the Omnipotent,
Today, I bow my head,
And raise my hands
Toward the Heavenly skies
As I pray for
My mind,
My body,
And my soul,
And for all humans who
Ask,
Seek,
And knock for a prayer,
To find hope and faith
As prayers are answered.
I keep my lantern of hope
Glowing upon Earth
Through the dark night
As I know You,
My God, the Omnipotent,
Have lit the stars as glowing lanterns,
For all Your creation
To find their ways

Through the dark
And frightful nights.
I pray during the hours of darkness,
And I pray for my inner soul
To never bid farewell
To hope and to faith,
As hope and faith
Are my support
Through the darkness
Into the light.
Within a few hours,
Everything changes.
From dusk, everything becomes darker.
Then, we find dawn
Smiling back at us.
As my prayers continue
For all the burdens
Of the last few hours
To be removed,
May blessings start pouring.
May all financial difficulties be eradicated.
May all physical and emotional illnesses
Be washed away
Through the glowing

Lights of prayers.
I hold on to my hope,
Renew my faith,
And watch the time change
From dusk to dawn.
As the clocks ring,
In front of me
Lies a new dawn.
Even then,
I, Your devoted creation,
With my head bowed down
And my hands locked in prayer,
Recite for one and for all,
To be released from
All the problems
Of the previous year,
And be washed
And cleansed
From all the troubles.
As the new glowing dawn
Burns out all obstacles
And sets us free
From all the troubles of the past,
We stand upon

A new bridge which takes all
To a new year
Filled with hope and blessings
For one and for all
As we travel to the next year.
Oh my God, my Creator,
I pray to You
For one and for all
To be happy,
Be safe, and accept all
Your humans as
Their human family.
As we cross over
To a new year
And as time changes,
We welcome hope and faith
Back into our lives
By lighting a candle of hope.
May we all say in union,
So be it,
As our prayers
Are accepted as
DAWN SMILES UPON US.

So Be It

DAWN THE FIRST MIRACLE OF THE DAY

Dusk appears all around
As I light my evening candles
To guide me until dawn.
Oh my God, my Creator,
I know darkness is ahead,
And the daylight hours
Are behind me.
I walk through
The dark night's
Lonely streets
With my evening candles
Glowing the path for me.
Above my head,
My God, my Creator,
Has lit the candles
Of the skies.
The glorious Moon shines
Upon my dark path,
As I keep steady
My evening candles.
I hear my inner self
Saying,

Never shall I fear
For my God is there.
Never shall I fall prey
To the dark temptations
For my Lord's
Commandments
Are my guide.
Never shall I go astray
As I only pray,
Worship,
And bow down to
My God the Omnipotent,
My God the Omnipresent,
My God the Omniscient.
All the obstacles
And all the hurdles of life,
I will survive
Through my faith.
As I hold on to
My glowing
Evening candles,
I keep alive
My blessed hope
And my blessed belief.

Through all the troubles of life,
My God is there.
Behind me are
The commandments
Of my God.
With me,
I have my faith.
Ahead of me,
I have my God,
My Creator,
Always standing over me.
My faith,
My belief,
And my love
For my God, my Creator,
Testify my God is always
Holding on to me
Through the darkest hours
As my God
Gifts me
The biggest miracle,
And I witness
DAWN THE FIRST MIRACLE OF THE DAY.

So Be It

DAWN THE FIRST WITNESS OF LIGHT

Oh my God,
This dark night's
Anger-filled ravishing words
Fly from the hearts
Of the mighty
And the powerful humans
To only darken the
Atmosphere of the weak,
The frail,
And the fearful.
Oh my God,
I know their flying words
Are not glowing stars
Trying to guide me.
They are not candles glowing
To help me.
The unjust anger,
The arrogant character traits,
And the ignorance
Of a person
Will neither hinder me,
Nor will they slow me down

As I have the glad tidings
And the lessons
Of my God, my Creator,
The Omnipotent.
I pray to You,
My God,
My Creator,
May my words of prayers
Be powered by
Love,
Peace,
And joy.
May my prayers guide all
Like glowing stars
Of the dark night's skies.
May my words be
Candles of hope.
May I, Your devotee,
Never recite words
Filled with anger.
May my lips always
Recite words of peace.
May my hands always be
In devotion of You.

May my feet
Only travel upon the path
You have blessed,
Not the path
You have forbidden.
Oh my God, my Creator,
May my prayers be
Compassionate.
May they be
My communication.
May I not be afraid
Of the harsh words
Of the people
Who spread
Hurtful words
As swords of destruction.
I pray oh my God,
Eternally hold on to me.
Let my words,
My prayers,
Rebuild a relation,
Not destroy.
I recite and teach
My mind,

My body,
And my soul
To ignore the harsh words
Yet not be the ignorant.
Let my words rebuild
The friendships
And the relationships on Earth
With
Love,
Peace,
And joy
As I hold on to hope
For a better tomorrow.
While I still walk
Within the dark
And frightful night,
I sense all shall be all right
As I see coming to me
With a smile,
With love, peace, and joy
Is my Creator's
Biggest star,
DAWN THE FIRST WITNESS OF LIGHT.

So Be It

DAWN TO APPEAR

Oh my God,
The Omnipotent,
Obstacles churn
All around me.
Freezing fears
Squeeze me.
Drowning and
Breathless I am
As darkness falls
All around.
I find
No helping hands
To hold
And give me a lift.
I find no words
To comfort
And save me
From drowning within
The vast ocean of obstacles.
Even then,
I hold on to my faith
In my God,

The Omnipotent.
I never fear
As my faith allows me
To believe
Even when
No one is near
And no one can hear,
My faith says
Why fear
As God is here.
Drowning in the ocean,
Burning above the Earth,
Breathless or breathing,
I will never fear
For I know
My God is here.
With faith,
I wait for the
Darkness of obstacles
To fade
As I pray
For
DAWN TO APPEAR.

So Be It

DAWN TO ERASE ALL ANGER

Oh my God,
My Creator,
I raise my hands
In acknowledgement
That
Pain,
Hurt,
Suffering,
Depression,
And stress cause
Misjudgment,
Misunderstanding,
And misguiding,
So, I, Your creation,
Ask, seek, and knock
For guidance from You,
My God,
The Giver and Taker of life.
As it is said in all the books,
Even in anger,
Do tremble
Yet do not sin.

So, I pray
To You,
My God,
My Creator,
For guidance.
Oh my God,
Take me to the truth,
The only truth,
To the door of knowledge,
And to the light.
May I, Your creation,
Who has devoted
My mind, body, and soul
To only You,
Not sin.
Oh the Merciful,
The Forgiver,
My God,
Remove the darkness from my soul.
Guide me out of the darkness
Guide me to the sunlight,
And allow
DAWN TO ERASE ALL ANGER.

So Be It

DAWN'S MORNING GRACE

My Lord, my Creator,
I walk upon a road
That leads to the houses
Of the rich
And the famous
Who have thrown
Away moldy bread
In their trash tonight as
They have too much.
They do not think
To share.
I land upon a path
Where I witness
A mother and a child
Going through trash
As they are hungry,
And the hunger
In their stomach
Will not let them sleep
On the cold,
Hard, and bare path,
They call home.

I shed tears as
I have
No bread,
No water,
And no change
To share.
There are so many people,
Yet I am alone,
Scared of them,
Your needy creation,
Who need my help.
Oh my Lord,
Forgive me
For I feel hopeless.
I have no money to give,
Yet I feel guilty.
I have
No extra clothes to share,
Yet I feel overdressed.
Oh my Lord,
Guide me,
Show me,
Let me know
What I can do

For Your needy creation.
Alone
And lonely at night,
I walk upon
A path divided
Through the rich,
The poor,
And the middle class.
How do I share
And give a helping hand
Without feeling
Scared or guilty?
I know soon
Dawn is going to
Peek through.
So, during the cold
And lonely night,
I pray,
May I be of help
To Your needy.
Oh my Lord,
As dawn reaches
My windows,
I realize I have my income.

I have a roof
Over my head.
I am able to work.
As I break bread,
I save one.
As I walk
By the same path today,
I can share
One loaf of bread.
I am blessed
For my Lord's grace
As I am able
To share and feed
A hungry soul,
A needy creation.
This is all
My Lord's blessings.
This is
My Lord's grace.
So today,
I pray and say,
Let this be my
DAWN'S MORNING GRACE.

So Be It

DESTINATION OF DAWN

Dear God,

As children send letters

To a saint

Through the faith of a child,

Their wishes, their prayers, and their hope

Remain intact

Through the parents' intercession.

Tonight, during the dark hours

Of a stormy night,

I, Your child,

With faith and hope

As my witnesses,

Am sending this prayer

As my inner wishes

My desires,

My innocent quests

To only You,

My God.

Where there is no one,

When there is no way out,

And only darkness engulfs

All that can be seen,

All that can be heard,
Or all that can be found,
In the midst of this,
I am lost.
I am lonely and I am scared.
My God,
As Your child, I cry to You.
I call on You.
I ask You to intercede for me,
Your creation, Your child.
Guide me.
Show me.
Place me where I am to be.
Give me the sustenance
To support myself.
Guide me to my twin flame,
And my twin flame to me
As You have blessed
The sacred bonds
Of a pure marriage.
My God, protect me tonight,
And give me the courage
For tomorrow.
Let me have the strength to forget

And forgive the wrong
And the wrongdoers of the past.
My God, bless me.
My God, hold me.
My God, support me during
This difficult period of my life.
Lift the storms away
From my path
And accept and answer
The prayers
I recite tonight
As I hope
With all my faith,
My prayers shall take me
To where I belong.
As dawn breaks open
And becomes
My traveling guide,
The brightest star,
The Sun,
Arrives with a smile
At his
DESTINATION OF DAWN.

So Be It

DEVOTIONAL SCALES OF DAWN

As darkness rises,
Fear grows.
I need Your guidance,
Oh my God, my Creator.
On this dark night
When everyone is right,
And no one accepts
They are wrong,
Who do I follow?
Where and from whom
Do I find my guidance?
So, I raise
My hands in prayer
As I seek
Forgiveness.
I ask for
My mind to be pure and clean.
I take responsibility
For myself,
For my mistakes,
And my wrongs.
Oh my God,

I follow the path
Glowing with hope,
Holding on to faith
As my guide.
I pray to You my God,
The Creator
Of all creation
Above and beyond,
To give me
Honor,
Dignity,
And courage.
May I not fall or be hurt
By the harsh
And wrongful
Voices of the wrong.
Oh my God,
Tonight,
As everyone tries to forget You,
My God,
The Omnipotent,
The Omnipresent,
May I be there
As a guiding lantern.

May my praying lanterns
Not take anyone
Off the right path.
May my guiding lanterns
Not blind anyone
But only be there
As a reminder,
Not to forget to pray.
As at the beginning,
When we were all created,
There was our Creator,
And as all shall end,
We will all return
To the one and only Creator
Only through His will
And at His time.
I pray,
May my prayers reach all
Who ask, seek, and knock
For forgiveness.
May my prayers
Give comfort
Within all souls
To never lose hope

As even when everything
And everyone leaves,
We still have our Creator,
The Omnipotent.
Today,
I pray
May I and all Your creation
Renew our faith,
Not in fear
Of the judgment scales,
But because
We love You,
My God, my Creator,
The Omnipotent.
I know throughout time,
You have
After the dark night's struggles,
Sent in the morning,
Your blessed and biggest star,
Your glowing Sun,
With messages and guidance
To be spread through the
DEVOTIONAL SCALES OF DAWN.

So Be It

ENTRANCE OF DAWN

Visionless fog covers up
The land,
The ocean,
And the mountains.
I, Your devotee,
Wait and pray for
The fog,
The hidden dangers,
And the known
And unknown obstacles
To evaporate.
Oh my God, my Creator,
I kneel
On my painful knees.
I bow
My dizzy head.
I raise
My frightened,
And quivering hands
In prayer.
I fill my lantern
With my last drops of oil,

And light
My trembling lantern
To guide myself.
I keep the path
I travel upon lit,
So, I,
Your devoted devotee,
Your blessed creation,
Do not fall asleep
Or fall prey
To the dark
Frightening night's
Fierce predators
Who loom around
Unannounced and unnoticed,
Searching for prey
To hunt,
To destroy,
And to remove innocence
Out of the innocent.
Oh my God, my Creator,
I pray for protection.
I pray for guidance.
I pray for a solution

To come
And appear
As the first door opens
From within
The fog-covered path.
Oh my God, my Creator,
I pray,
May the oil
Within my lantern
Last until
All the fog,
All the obstacles,
And all the troubles
Of my life
Disappear,
As my God,
The Omnipotent,
The Omnipresent,
The Omniscient,
Opens
The door of opportunities
At the first
ENTRANCE OF DAWN.

So Be It

EQUALLY AT DAWN

Oh my God,
The Omnipotent,
Tonight,
I sit on my knees
And pray
For all Your creation
As I see
There are kings
And there are paupers.
There are the rich
And there are the poor.
People have castles
And then people live
On the streets.
People throw away food
As there is too much,
Yet I hear children cry
As they go to bed hungry.
Oh my God, my Creator,
I pray
For all Your creation
To have food,

Have shelter,
Have clothes,
Have dignity,
And have honor.
As we only worship
And salute You,
My God, my Creator,
Let not another human
Go hungry
Or get wet on the streets,
Or be destitute
As we, all the humans,
Are Your creation.
Traveling through life,
We pray to You
Through this blessed prayer
For help and protection,
And for all our struggles to end
With Your will.
My God,
My Creator,
Pick us up
From the long hurdle-filled path
And place us all

Upon the path where
There is no superior,
No inferior,
No rich,
And no poor.
All are just
Your blessed creation
Who recite
This blessed prayer to You.
You are
Our Creator
Whom
We worship
And we pray to.
You are
Our Creator
Who has said
You treat all equally.
We too will
With a blessed prayer
After our lesson is learned,
Treat all
EQUALLY AT DAWN.

So Be It

ERASE DARKNESS WITH DAWN

My God,
My Creator,
Help me with all my worries,
My stress,
And my anxiety.
I know faith is believing,
Not doubting.
I know it is the seed of doubt
Versus faith.
So, I choose to
Believe in my faith.
I believe You,
The Alpha and the Omega
Will erase all my troubles away.
Oh my God, I have faith.
Oh my God, I believe.
Oh my God, I will not worry but pray.
May all my troubles be erased
As You,
The Alpha and the Omega,
ERASE DARKNESS WITH DAWN.

So Be It

EXHORTATION AT DAWN

My God,
The Creator,
The Destructor,
The Giver,
The Taker,
Your creation upon Earth
Are suffering.
As fire erupts on the hills,
It spreads and takes all
On its way
For it has no mercy.
My God, my Creator,
As human lives are lost,
Beloved animals run in fear
As they try to find shelter.
Humans try to protect
Their homes,
Their families,
Their friends,
And strangers
As all within vision
Are burning to ashes.

My God, have mercy.
My God, the Merciful,
When and where
Everything is lost,
Hope is found.
With faith and hope,
We call upon You
For within Your hands
All is.
As I rest my faith
And hope in You,
Nothing is lost,
For even when everything
Becomes ashes,
Faith rises higher than
The burning flames.
As we carry
Our candles of hope
Within our inner souls,
We awaken faith
Through hope.
The burning fires
Of the dark night's skies
Are nothing

Compared to our burning
Candles of hope
As we have our hope and faith,
The gifts of our God,
The Creator,
The Omnipotent,
The Omnipresent.
On this frightful burning night,
We see upon the skies,
The full Moon,
A gift from our Creator
Reminding us
To never lose hope,
And to never lose faith.
For with hope and faith,
I know
My God is there.
I know
My God never left me.
Even when there were houses
Filled with laughter and life,
My God was there.
Tonight, as there is nothing,
But burned ashes and memories,

My God is there.
Everything begins and ends
At my God's will and mercy.
So, we, the beloved creation,
Of the beloved Omnipotent
Will rise again
At the mercy and blessings of
My God, my Creator,
As long as we carry
Within our bags of life,
Hope and faith.
For where there is hope,
My God, my Creator,
Is there.
From this night's full Moon,
We shall find ourselves
Upon another new day,
Where our prayers
Will be answered
As we say at the first sight of light,
With hope, faith, and complete devotion,
Our
EXHORTATION AT DAWN.

So Be It

FIRST CALLS OF DAWN

My God, have mercy.
My God, protect me
From the sins of this time.
Oh my God, I walk alone
With Your commandments.
I conceal within my mind,
My body, and my soul,
Repentance and redemption
As I ask, I seek, and I knock
For forgiveness.
I ask for Your guidance.
I seek Your mercy.
I knock for Your protection.
May my mind, my body, and my soul
Be sin free.
May I never go astray
Or fall prey
To the temptations
Of this world,
For I float alone
In the vast sinful ocean,
Where all I see is darkness.

No stars above are guiding.
No arks in the vast ocean are guiding.
Oh my God, have mercy.
Show me the direction
As I float alone
In the dark freezing ocean,
Where the water is muddy
And covered with tempting sins.
All that is wrong
By Your commandments
Are performed and protected
By the powerful voices
Of the wrong.
I am a lonely swimmer
In the dark night's
Freezing ocean,
Floating in uncharted waters.
Darkness prevails here.
The stars of Heavens above
Are forgotten
As the only stars are
The dark unlit ones on Earth.
They do not shine
The path for me,

Nor do they guide
All lost and stranded souls
In the dark muddy ocean.
My God,
In this dark, freezing, muddy ocean,
I am lost.
I am cold.
My lips are frozen.
My body can barely float.
I seek guidance,
I knock for answers,
And I ask for directions
From only You.
Even when lost and stranded,
And alone on this Earth,
I have my lips which pray
As my connection to You
Is never lost
Even in the freezing night's
Dark ocean.
I have You
Through my prayer calls.
I have You
Through my recitation of prayers

That shall never stop
Calling upon You.
They are my strength.
They are my way.
They are my guiding lights
Until dawn breaks open.
Through my blessed prayers,
I shall find my answers
For in my prayers,
I see
My God the Merciful,
My God the Forgiver,
My God the Most Kind,
My God the Most Loving.
My God sends me signs that
My prayers are answered.
My God has sent His brightest star,
His remover of darkness,
To guide me
And protect me.
Even when all seems lost,
Even when hope seems lost,
Even when faith seems weak and lost,
My Creator,

My God,

Never leaves me.

He always sends

At the end of

The darkest hour,

His brightest star.

I am reminded

My God,

The Omnipotent,

Never left me

Throughout my trials, failures,

Or successes.

I witness

The first miracle

Of the day

When dawn breaks open

Through the dark skies.

I, a blessed soul,

With realization

My prayers have been

Answered,

Witness the

FIRST CALLS OF DAWN.

So Be It

FIRST GRACE AT DAWN

Oh my God,
You are my only hope.
From dusk through dawn,
I walk through
The obstacles of life.
Without any direction, any guide,
And no one to hold my hands
To guide me
To my destination,
I pray only to You.
I light my lantern of hope
To guide myself through the dark paths
As I witness a miracle of the night skies,
The blinking stars.
I pray only to You.
Guide me.
Help me.
Oh my God,
May I find my way
Back to You.
To help my glowing prayer lantern,
You have lit

All the lanterns in the skies.
I pray only to You,
My God,
The Omnipotent,
To protect me
From all the known
And unknown dangers
Looming around my life
That I cannot see, feel, or hear,
Yet You, my God,
Know all about.
So, I pray only to You.
As I cross the dark night and witness
The first glimpse of light
Fighting to peek through
The dark skies,
I kneel on my knees,
Bow my head,
And pray only to You.
I pray for health, wealth,
And wisdom.
I pray to be safe
Throughout the day,
Throughout the night,

And all throughout my life
On this blessed Earth.
May I, Your devoted creation,
Always be on Your path,
The path blessed only by You.
May I not fall prey
Upon the wrong path condemned
By You, my God,
The Omnipotent,
The Omnipresent,
The Omniscient.
I pray until
I witness the biggest miracle.
After the dark night's
Frightening journey,
The biggest star appears
With a smile upon Your Earth,
Your blessed morning star,
Your Sun.
I take my blessings and recite
My prayers to You
As I give my
FIRST GRACE AT DAWN.

So Be It

FIRST KISS OF DAWN

Darkness covers
All around me.
Fear grips my inner soul.
In the quiet dark night,
The only sounds
That can be heard
Far or near,
Are my own heartbeats.
My mind, my body,
And my soul
Knock for a break.
My eyes seek
To escape
As my feet try to run
When I fear,
Yet I still am stuck
In the same place.
I ask for help,
Yet words fail.
My tears roll out,
Yet miss everyone's eyes.
I see

My Lord's first glimmer of hope
Sparks the night skies.
I hear
My Lord's breath
Through the gentle winds.
I feel
My Lord's embrace
Through the sweet fragrances
Of the moonflowers
Blooming under
The Moon's glow.
The waterdrops
From the morning dew
Touch my feet.
During
The dark night's struggles,
Everyone leaves,
But my Lord is here.
No one knows
I am in pain,
But my Lord knows.
No one answers my calls,
But my Lord glows
All around me.

As I walk
Out of the darkness
And into the light,
I welcome the
New beginnings
As I know
The past is gone.
The future is mine.
The present is a gift
I must embrace.
My prayers reach
The Heavenly skies
As darkness disappears
And I see my Lord's
Biggest star.
Answering my prayers,
My Lord gifts me
A kiss,
A blessing,
A prayer answered
Through
The
FIRST KISS OF DAWN.

So Be It

FIRST LIGHT OF DAWN

My God,
The Omnipotent,
The Creator,
The Punisher,
The Forgiver,
The Most Loving,
And the Most Kind,
I, Your creation,
With all my mind, my body,
And my eternal soul,
Ask, seek, and knock
Upon Your mercy to guide me
And to protect me.
May You,
My God, the Omnipotent,
Remove all my hurdles,
All my hindrances,
And all the barriers
That keep me
From going to the place I must go,
From being the person I must be,
And from all the achievements I must achieve

Through this life.
Oh my God,
The Omnipotent,
I pray to You and only You,
The Giver,
The Taker,
And the Creator of destiny.
Oh my God,
I raise my hands
Tonight and forever
Through a pure and blessed prayer,
To be blessed and eternally upon
The path You have blessed,
And to never go astray or get lost
From the path You have blessed.
I am Your beloved creation
And You, my God,
Are the Guide and my salvation.
So, I pray and hope
With protection from this blessed prayer,
May all my obstacles
Be burned to ashes through the
FIRST LIGHT OF DAWN.

So Be It

FIRST SIGHT OF DAWN

Oh my God,
At sundown,
I set out to watch the amazing twilight.
Yet my God, I shiver
As realization crawls into my heart,
Nightfall has approached.
Oh my God,
I must not forget to pray.
I place my hands together.
I look up toward the dark skies.
With complete devotion, I pray.
Oh my God,
May I not get lost or bring upon
My mind, body, and soul,
The deadly sins of
Pride,
Greed,
Lust,
Envy,
Gluttony,
Wrath,
And

Sloth.
Oh my God,
There is darkness all around me,
Yet my prayers are
My candles of hope
Glowing within the dark.
My prayers keep safe within me,
The Heavenly virtues of
Faith,
Hope,
Charity,
Prudence,
Justice,
Temperance,
And courage.
As my virtues embrace me,
They keep me safe
From the sins of the twilight hours.
I fear not the dark as I never forget to pray.
I bravely walk out from the twilight hours
As I catch
The
FIRST SIGHT OF DAWN.

So Be It

FIRST SIGHT OF LIGHT AT DAWN

Oh my God,
The Omnipotent,
As the first sight
Of darkness overshadows
My part of the world,
I fear not anything
As I forget not my Creator.
Through everything,
I only worship You.
Oh my God, my Creator,
Throughout all the troubles
Over the journey of my life,
I, Your blessed creation,
Never forget You,
As for You,
My God, my Creator,
I stay away
From the forbidden sins.
I avoid the evil temptations
Sent my way.
Throughout
My journey on Earth,

I only worship You.
Oh my God, my Creator,
My eyes open at dawn
As with my first breath of the day,
I say,
Glory be to my Lord.
As the Sun sets,
I, the traveler of life,
Try to find my way
Out of the obstacles,
The hurdles,
And the burdens of life.
I say to You,
May I, Your creation,
For myself
And all other lost travelers
Behind me,
Carry the candles of hope
Until my God, my Creator,
The Omnipotent,
Sends to us His creation,
The
FIRST SIGHT OF LIGHT AT DAWN.

So Be It

FIRST SPARKLES OF DAWN

Oh my God,
Tonight, I kneel and pray
Only to You.
As I turn within an ocean
Of obstacles,
May I not be
Blinded by fear
Or clouded by my own mind,
As I have You.
I have my faith
Which is victorious
Against all the fears combined.
I will swim across the ocean
As I know Your hands
Will be my canoe.
I will climb the mountain
As Your hands will
Be my stairs.
I will not fear
My destiny,
My fate,
Or my path

As You walk with me
Through everything.
Oh my God, my Creator,
I will walk
With my eyes open.
I will try to do my best,
Yet when I fall,
And when life fails me,
I will not fear
As I know
I have You.
I fear not the darkness
As I know
My God, my Creator,
Walks with me
With a candle in His hands
Only to light my path.
Through my eternal faith,
I know throughout my life,
My God carries me
From the dark night to
The
FIRST SPARKLES OF DAWN.

So Be It

FORESIGHT OF DAWN

Oh my God,
The Creator of all creations,
All living and non-living things,
The Earth,
The Heavens above,
And beyond,
Tonight,
I and all Your creations
Walk over yet
To another earthly year.
The night turns dark.
The clocks announce it is midnight.
It is announced the year has changed.
The skies above
And the Earth beneath are the same,
Yet peace, joy, and laughter
Fly from people to people.
The feeling of love and affection
Spread in the air.
The skies glow
With glimmering colors of lights.
The Earth is filled with music.

I watch all in union
Celebrate with hope and faith.
Everything will be all right
As we have our God,
The Omnipotent,
The Omnipresent,
The Omniscient.
Our God guides us through love, joy, and laughter,
To enjoy today,
To enjoy tonight,
And to not drown ourselves in sorrows,
But forget all our troubles,
Forget all our obstacles,
And believe in the Omnipotent's
Grace, mercy, and forgiveness.
We should always remember
Troubles come
And obstacles appear,
Yet solutions too are found
Through hope and faith.
So, as I find myself
In the new year,
With renewed hope and faith,
I place all my worries,

All my troubles,
And all my fears
In Your hands,
My God, my Creator.
I believe now,
I can worry less as everything is
In my God's hands,
As they always were
And always shall be.
I shall with hope and faith
Preplan my days and my nights.
I shall walk on my own feet,
And I shall use my own hands
To complete my work on Earth.
Yet I pray to You,
My God, my Creator,
To always guide me,
Protect me,
And hold on to me
Through the hardest times,
So, I do not fall
Until I find my safe grounds.
Oh my God,
Through this life and beyond,

Never let me go
As I shall never let go of
My faith and my hope.
Oh my God,
Help me
And all who have walked
Over to a new year
With our resolutions
As we plan
And try to walk in the dark,
Waiting for a glimpse of hope
From the biggest star
To guide us and show us
Which way,
How,
And where we are to go.
As we walk in the dark,
Oh my God, my Creator,
For the right direction,
The right path,
And the right decision,
I pray at the first sight of dawn for the
FORESIGHT OF DAWN.

So Be It

FORGIVEN AT DAWN

Oh my God,
My heart is filled with fear.
I am afraid as
The unwanted and unexpected
Burdens drown
My mind,
My body,
And my soul.
Oh my God, my Creator,
As dusk falls
And darkness enters
My part of the world,
I shiver in fear.
I see sins flood the streets.
I hear how everyone
Is committing these sins.
They proclaim through their voices,
These are accepted
And are all normal
To be committed in the dark.
They talk about them
As the normal oath of life

In daylight hours.
All the forbidden sins
Proclaimed by You,
My God,
As the deadly sins,
Are being committed widely
Yet my God,
Why then did You say
They are forbidden?
Why do the wrong people
Convince all that the wrong is right,
And the right is wrong?
Oh my God,
As I raise these issues,
I am belittled.
I am being made to feel ashamed
Because I follow
Your commandments.
I try to walk upon Your path.
I collect all my known and unknown sins
In prayer beads
And I send them out for forgiveness.
I send them out for redemption.
I repent

Through my mind,
My body,
And my soul
To never let the sins
Of the powerful and mighty
Touch me even when my feet
Touch the high waves
Flooding the Earth
From the sinners' committed sins.
I know I must not judge.
I must not say what is right
Or wrong as all creation
Are the judged
As You, my God, my Creator,
Are the only Judge.
Neither shall I speak ill of anyone,
Nor shall I let others take me astray through life.
I am the traveler who shall
Not be tempted,
Not fall prey to the tempting sins
Of the dark and lost path,
Not normalize the sins as accepted,
And not complain about
Or accept the force of the wrong waves

Of the rising sea waters.
I shall stand by the same sea
And let my prayers wash my feet.
I shall let the fresh and pleasant breeze
Of the dark night
Wipe away all my fears.
I shall repent, redeem, and awaken
From all the confusion,
And remember
With clear consciousness,
My prayers are my guide
Through all the dark night's confusion.
I know my God, my Creator,
Hears everything,
Sees everything,
And knows everything.
As I see
The first sight of light,
I know my earthly vehicle,
Will not become a lost creation,
As through my prayers,
I am the
FORGIVEN AT DAWN.

So Be It

FROM DUSK TO DAWN

Oh my God,
My Creator,
I pray for salvation.
I pray for protection.
I pray with devotion.
I pray not so You
Hear or answer me,
But my God,
I pray
So I can
Hear and feel You.
Oh my God,
My Creator,
May my prayers be
My saving grace
As within my prayers,
I find You.
My God,
My Creator,
I pray
With my mind,
My body,

And my soul,
To find You.
Within my mind,
My body,
And my soul,
I have my words
From my prayers
Like the prayer beads
To pray nonstop
And
To hold on to
Through darkness
And through dawn.
When
I find You,
Oh my God,
I will have then
Found
My salvation,
My protection,
And my devotion
As I pray
FROM DUSK TO DAWN.

So Be It

FUTURE BLESSES FROM DAWN

Oh my God,
I pray tonight
As I walk on the path of the present,
With me as my guide,
I have the lessons of my past.
As I walk crossing the star-filled night,
I pray to You,
My God, my Creator,
To guide me in the direction
Which is not covered with thorns
But covered with Your blessings.
With my faith,
My hope,
And my belief
In You, my God, my Creator,
I pray You bless me
As I know what is not known to me
Is known to You.
Tonight, my God bless me
So my
FUTURE BLESSES FROM DAWN.

So Be It

GLOWING DAWN

Oh my God,
The Omnipotent,
Guide me,
Hold me,
Protect me
As I walk through
The bridge of obstacles,
And as I cross the river of crocodiles.
Oh my God,
Remove all my worries.
Oh my God,
Remove all my stress.
Oh my God,
Remove all my doubt
And allow my faith,
My hope,
And my belief to guide me
Through the difficulties I face.
Oh my God,
Let my faith be my eyes.
Let my vision of Your hands holding mine
And my feet following Your blessed footsteps

Be my saving grace.
Oh my God,
Tonight,
As I walk through the darkest path,
May my prayers
Recited through my mind,
My body,
And my soul
Be my candles of hope
As I walk
Out from the darkest
Place in my life
Only by holding on to You,
My God, my Creator
The Omnipotent.
I know You,
My God,
Wipe away all darkness
From my life
As You gift me with
The first glory of
The
GLOWING DAWN.

So Be It

GOOD HEALTH SPREADS THROUGH DAWN

Darkness covers the light
As the Sun sets,
Yet I,
Your creation,
Ask, seek, and knock
To be well,
To be healthy,
To be healed
From all the illnesses,
All the health problems,
And all the physical pain
This earthly vehicle picks up.
Oh my God,
My Creator,
As I walk
Through the dark night's path,
I pray for a
Healthy mind,
Healthy body,
And healthy soul,
So I can
With harmony and blessings

Finish all
The blessed work
You, my God,
My Creator,
Have sent me to accomplish.
You have promised
To help guide and uphold
All through
The journey of life.
With this prayer,
I ask
Not to give
What I cannot take,
But help me with
All that I can.
I pray to be blessed
With good health
As I know
My God bestows upon me
This miracle
As nightfall passes by
And
GOOD HEALTH SPREADS THROUGH DAWN.

So Be It

GRACE OF DAWN

As dawn breaks through
And the Sun shines upon all creation,
May the Sun's rays burn away
All physical, emotional, spiritual,
And any other type of obstacles.
Oh my God,
I, Your creation,
Pray for mercy, forgiveness, and blessings.
I, Your creation,
Seek the right path which
Leads to Your grace, mercy, and blessings.
Oh my God,
Hold my hands as day becomes dusk.
Guide me through the dark nights.
Show me the light
Which bursts through the dark skies
And shines its amber light upon Earth.
Oh my God,
Bless me again with
The
GRACE OF DAWN.

So Be It

GRATITUDE FROM DAWN

Night falls
Across the land
As I give my grace
For the food
I have on my plate,
The warm clothing
On my body,
And the safe bed
I sleep within.
Oh my God,
I give grace
For this life,
For this Earth,
For the Moon,
And for the stars
That guide all of us
Out of darkness
To the biggest star
Of my God.
I give my
GRATITUDE FROM DAWN.

So Be It

GUIDE ME TO DAWN

My God, my Creator,
All around me,
Darkness covers the light.
Confusion covers the messages.
Misguidance covers the paths.
So, I place my hands together.
With my mind, body, and soul
Devoted in devotion
Of my God, my Creator,
I pray with complete faith.
With my candles of hope, I remove the darkness.
With knowledge, I read the true messages.
With direction, I find my path.
I let my mistakes,
My wrong turns,
And my failures
Not take me astray
Or away from You,
My God, my Creator,
But be my lessons of dusk to
GUIDE ME TO DAWN.

So Be It

GUIDING FOOTPRINTS TOWARD DAWN

Oh my God, my Creator,
The Sun has set in the vast skies.
Darkness falls all around.
I ask,
I seek,
And I knock
For directions,
For guidance,
For the path I must be upon.
Oh my God,
Where do I find a guide?
Who will help me with directions?
Why, my God,
Can I not see any help?
I stand,
I kneel,
I bow,
And I open my eyes toward the skies
As I keep praying.
Then, I witness the guiding stars
And the bright shining Moon
Of the night skies

Glow and show me
My own footprints
Which I left behind.
I knew only then,
To get out of this darkness,
I must create my own path
As I have the glad tidings of my God,
The Omnipotent.
So, I pray to my God,
For You are my Creator,
The Omnipotent.
I pray for all Your creation
Not to be left alone in this darkness
Like I was.
Tonight, I shall become
A guide,
A help,
And a map
As for myself
And all who are lost like me,
I must create
The
GUIDING FOOTPRINTS TOWARD DAWN.

So Be It

HAPPY AND BLESSED NEW DAWN

Oh my God,
As I open my eyes
To another day,
I realize
Blessed I am
I have today.
Blessed I am
I have another chance.
Blessed I am
As today I will repent,
Redeem,
And awaken
All over again.
I pray from my mind,
Body,
And soul
To my God, my Creator,
The Omnipotent,
The Omnipresent,
The Omniscient,
For better health,
Better wealth,

And better wisdom
To live on this Earth
As per Your wish
On Your path,
Through Your commandments.
Oh my God,
May I never go astray
Or fall prey to the wrongdoers
And the wrong path.
Oh my God,
Hold on to me.
Give me support.
Show me the way
To travel through the day
And the dark nights
With dignity,
Courage,
And
Respect
As I within Your grace,
Travel through the dark nights
To another
HAPPY AND BLESSED NEW DAWN.

So Be It

HEALING FOUNTAIN OF DAWN

The skies are pouring upon
And drenching the Earth.
A ravishing angry thunderstorm
Is making life hard.
My Lord, the Omnipotent,
Help me, the faithful,
The lost and stranded creation.
Through all the obstacles of life,
I am drenched in rain.
Waiting for a miraculous break tonight
From Heavens above,
I am shivering from the cold.
I ask You my Lord, the Omnipotent,
Why is it I feel like
I always suffer?
I am always forgotten.
I find myself within
Financial, physical, and emotional distress.
I try to walk forward,
But find huge boulders
On my path.
I try to walk backward,

But realize time only walks forward.
How do I get out of this hurdle
Life unjustly placed upon me?
Even when You forget me,
Or place me on the hardest roads
On Earth,
My Lord, the Omnipotent,
I will eternally keep
Your name upon my lips.
I shall hold on to my faith.
As I close my eyes,
I shall imagine You are here with me
For my faith never falters.
Eternally You, my Lord, the Omnipotent,
Are always within my soul.
This physical body
Shall keep walking forward
With faith in You,
My Lord, the Omnipotent.
Through all the storms of life,
Through all the hurdles,
I will never give up
My faith in You.
I know You will eventually

Turn around and see me.
You will hear my knocks.
You will answer my prayers
As my recitation of
These blessed and sacred prayers
Will keep on beating
As long as my heart beats.
My Lord, the Omnipotent,
I believe in You.
I believe whatever You do
Is for my good.
Whatever You decide
Is my blessed path,
My destination, and my destiny.
My prayers, my faith,
And my glowing candles
That I burn in Your name,
Will guide me through
The hardest periods of my life.
I witness daylight break through
Even as the skies
Are drenching the Earth.
My Lord, the Omnipotent,
During a thunderstorm,

I realize even the rain
That refuses to stop
Is nothing but Your love
And Your blessings
Pouring down from Heavens above.
It is preventing me
From traveling upon the wrong path,
The path You have cursed
As I wait upon the path
You have blessed.
As You teach me to be patient
And never lose faith,
My prayers too
Will find their answers.
You have,
After a dark night's frightful storm,
Opened for me,
Your creation,
As Your blessings and Your love,
Through the rainstorm
From Heavens above,
The
HEALING FOUNTAIN OF DAWN.

So Be It

HEALTHY BY DAWN

Oh my God,
The Omnipotent,
Tonight,
I pray for
All of Your creation
Who are not well
As the mind is foggy,
The soul is unsettled,
And the body feels unwell.
I pray to You,
My God,
My Creator,
The Healer,
And the Remover
Of all hurdles,
Of all pain,
And of all sufferings.
My God,
Heal all,
Hold all,
And help all
As they ask,

They seek,
And they knock upon
Your door of mercy
To be physically healed
From all illnesses.
You are the Creator.
You are the Savior.
You are the Healer.
For when and where
There is no hope,
There is no way,
There is no path,
And there is no solution,
You are there
For all of Your creation.
With Your blessed hands,
You created all.
I ask
On Your mercy,
For those who pray
And believe in miracles
Of the Omnipotent
To be healed
By Your blessed hands.

We, Your devoted creation,
Never let go of
Our faith.
We never let go of
Our hope.
We never let go of
Our belief.
Even when there is no one,
Our God,
The Creator,
The Omnipotent,
The Omnipresent,
The Omniscient,
Is there.
With complete faith,
We, Your devoted creation,
Believe with this prayer
Recited all night,
From our mind,
Our body,
And our soul,
We shall be
HEALTHY BY DAWN.

So Be It

ILLUMINATION AT DAWN

Life's journey takes me through
The dark and dangerous path,
Where I freeze in fear.
I try to get out
And walk toward the light,
Yet only a few steps at a time,
As the frightful obstacles
Have placed a heavy burden
Upon my path.
My road ahead is there,
Yet covered with hurdles.
Oh my God, help me.
Oh my God,
The Caretaker of this life,
I stand within this darkness
With courage, faith, and hope,
Knowing I have You
In the darkness,
Walking with me.
If only I could see You,
My God, my Creator.
If only I could hear You,

My God, my Creator.
Yet my faith hears You.
My hope sees You.
My courage allows me to continue
One step at a time.
As I walk through the darkness,
I see the candles
You have lit
Even in the dark skies for me.
I witness the dark path
Around me,
Glowing from
The moonshine,
Sending me secret messages
To never lose hope
Even when all is dark
And all is lost.
Faith and hope in You,
My God, my Creator,
Keep me
Going forward.
I know even in this darkness,
I will find You.
Through my faith,

And my belief,
I will always have You.
I know my God,
My Creator,
Ahead of my journey, I have You.
Behind my journey,
I have the learned lessons of life.
Yet during this journey,
I know I have with me,
My prayer calls.
Throughout everything
Each day and each night,
I send out to You
My sacred,
Innocent,
And heartfelt
Prayer calls which You answer.
I see in front of me,
Wiping all the darkness,
And shattering the glass doors of darkness,
Appears the biggest and brightest star,
With
ILLUMINATION AT DAWN.

So Be It

INSPIRATION OF DAWN

May I the traveler,
Walking through this life,
Never forget You,
My God, my Creator.
May I never lose hope,
Never give up on my faith,
Never go astray,
And never walk away
From Your blessed path.
As I walk through
The obstacles of life,
Physical, emotional,
And financial hurdles
Keep placing me off
Your blessed path of life.
Oh my God,
My Creator,
During this dark night,
I pray for guidance.
I pray for sustenance.
I pray for good health.
I pray for love,

And I pray for a miracle
To come true.
As I raise my hands
In prayer only to You,
My God, my Creator,
Accept my prayers
As I recite them
Only to You.
Oh my God, my Creator,
I believe the dark and frightful path
Will end
As I keep calling You,
My God, my Creator.
With this prayer,
I, Your devoted creation,
Call upon You
On this dark night.
Guide me and all
Who call You
Through a prayer
To land upon the right path,
The path where You my God
Have blessed us
With financial sustenance,

With complete healing of the mind,
The body, and the soul,
Where blessings come
And unite twin flames
Into one home
Of holy matrimony,
And where children find
Love and harmony,
And are blessed with
A happy family.
Oh my God,
On this dark night
Where no light can be seen,
I find hope through the twinkles
Of the faraway stars
Glowing above my lonely path.
I see hope glowing
In the dark night's skies.
I hold on to my faith,
And my prayers,
As I know I shall pray
Through the whole night
For a breakthrough.
With the first sight of light,

I find my prayers
Are being answered
As I never gave up
On my faith
And my hope
That my God, my Creator,
Answers all prayers
Of those devotees who
Never give up.
I walk out
From this dark night's
Lost and lonely path,
Holding on to my prayers.
I know
My God, my Creator,
Has answered my prayers,
Through the first sight of dawn.
From this day forth,
I shall eternally
Call this blessed prayer
I send above the Heavenly skies,
My
INSPIRATION OF DAWN.

So Be It

INTERCESSION FROM DAWN

The skies turn dark
As the Sun sets
Upon the Heavenly skies.
Oh my God, my Creator,
I raise my hands
For all Your creation
To find within
Their minds, bodies, and souls,
Love, hope, and understanding
Through faith, belief, and knowledge.
My God, my Creator,
We the humans
Are all Your creation.
On this dark, fearful, and confused night,
Accept my prayers.
Guide the lost.
Show the way to You.
As I pray for all,
Let my prayers
Be an
INTERCESSION FROM DAWN.

So Be It

JOURNEY FROM DUSK TO DAWN

Darkness grips me
In fear,
Placing
A blanket of uncertainty
Over me.
The dark night's pouring rain
Freezes my feet.
The thunder
And the lightning
Frighten me.
Yet my God,
I, Your creation,
Still hold on to my faith,
My hope,
And my belief.
Even within confusion,
Within uncertainty,
And within gripping fear,
I still walk forward
Through the dark night's path
For I know
My God,

My Creator,

Is there.

My mind,

My body,

And my soul

Believe my God

Will never leave me.

Within this frightening darkness,

I hold on to

My faith,

My hope,

And my belief

In my God,

The Omnipotent.

I pray

With complete faith,

Complete hope,

And complete belief,

My God will

Never leave me

And will accompany me

On my

JOURNEY FROM DUSK TO DAWN.

So Be It

LESSONS OF LIFE AT DAWN

Oh my God, my Creator,
I learn to be patient.
I learn to be humble.
I learn to be kind.
I learn to be giving.
I learn to be honest.
I learn to never give up
Traveling through the dark night
Through the obstacles
Of my life.
My God, my Creator,
Always sends messages
Through His guiding lights.
My God teaches me
Through His guiding lights,
The nightmares will be over.
Yet only those who have learned
To be patient,
Humble,
Kind,
Giving,
And honest

Through the dark nights,
And waited for
Dawn to break through,
Will see life is a blessing.
Oh my God, my Creator,
I, Your devoted creation,
Shall wait through
The dark nights
As I know
Dawn will break through
Within my life soon.
My work soon
Will be over,
As I shall soon see
The first light
Of Your brightest star,
The Sun's amber glow.
All the difficulties
And all the trials
You have placed us through
Shall be over
As we graduate through the
LESSONS OF LIFE AT DAWN.

So Be It

LET DAWN'S GLORY BE

Oh my God, my Creator,
I walk into a church.
All ask me,
Who,
What,
Where,
And
Why am I there?
Oh my God,
As I walk into a temple,
All ask me,
Who,
What,
Where,
And
Why am I there?
Oh my God,
Who,
What,
Where,
And
Why

Must I answer a human
Who,
What,
Where,
And
Why
My heart seeks only You.
Oh my God,
Who,
What,
Where,
And
Why
Must I answer the humans
Who do not understand?
Oh my God,
My prayers are not for
Who,
What,
Where,
And
Why.
Oh my God,
Let my prayers reach You

Even though I have
No churches,
No temples,
And
No walls
To protect me
But only You.
So, I pray
To whom?
To You my God.
For What?
For mercy my God.
Where?
Within Your invisible temple my God.
And
Why?
As I am welcomed only there my God.
So, I pray
To You my God
To remove all the darkness
From this world,
And my God,
LET DAWN'S GLORY BE.

So Be It

LET THERE BE DAWN

Oh my God,
My Creator,
The Omnipotent,
Today,
I pray for healing.
Oh my God,
My Creator,
Remove my fears.
Oh my God,
My Creator,
Remove my obstacles.
Oh my God,
My Creator,
Remove my worries.
These grave obstacles
Have become the
Partners of my life.
Oh my God,
My Creator,
Remove my burdens
And let me breathe in
Positive vibes,

Positive energies,
And positive thoughts.
All my heavy burdens
Disappear through the touch
Of Your blessed hands.
You remove darkness
From this Earth
At the end
Of each dark night
As the biggest star,
The Sun,
Breaks through
With Your commands.
I pray to You,
My God,
My Creator,
The Omnipotent,
With mercy, grace,
And blessings,
Remove all the
Troubles of my life,
And even in my life,
LET THERE BE DAWN.

So Be It

MANIFEST DAWN AFTER DARK

Oh my God,
My Creator,
Tonight,
I raise my hands
And I pray.
I believe
My affirmations
And my positive thoughts,
All will not just
Be a dream
But will be my reality.
My faith and my hope
Will convert my dreams
Into my reality
As I positively affirm
My thoughts,
My wishes,
And my words into prayers.
Oh my God,
My Creator,
Grant me the ability
To worship

And to complete my journey
As I ask You
To accept my prayer requests.
I ask You,
My God,
My Creator,
To grant me
The ability
To visualize and affirm
My beliefs
And my prayers
Into reality.
Oh my God,
My Creator,
I know
You have answered
My prayers
As I remain steadfast.
With Your command,
Oh my God,
My Creator,
You will
MANIFEST DAWN AFTER DARK.

So Be It

MAY DAWN'S GLORY BE

My God, my Creator,
As the Sun sets,
And the world
Becomes dark,
We,
Your devoted creation,
All ask,
Seek,
And knock
For
Some light of hope.
May I,
And all Your creation
Who ask,
Seek,
And knock
On Your door,
Not fall prey
Or go astray
Within the
Lost
Forbidden paths,

The paths that light up
With temptations
And with the forbidden sins
Of the wrong.
Oh my God, my Creator,
As Your Sun
Travels far away,
As we the creation
On Earth move,
I try to find my way
Through the hurdles
Of the dark night.
I pray with
All my faith,
My hope,
My mind,
My body,
And my soul
To be protected
And to be safe
From all the obstacles
And the dark
And dangerous
Predators of Earth

And beyond.
Hold on to me.
Protect me.
Keep me within
Your embrace.
Through my prayers,
My faith,
And my love
For You, my God,
Guide me
Through Your,
Blinking night stars,
And Your Moon's true glory
Until I can be under
The amber glow of Your Sun
As then,
I will again raise my hands
And pray.
With all my faith
And all my hope,
I will recite
Until the Sun sets again,
MAY DAWN'S GLORY BE.

So Be It

MAY THERE BE DAWN

I pray to my God,
As dusk approaches,
May I, Your creation,
Be good and be safe.
Oh my God,
May I not go astray or fall prey
To temptations and forbidden sins.
May I walk through the dark nights
With dignity, grace, and honor,
As I know when and where
Nothing can be seen,
Nothing can be felt,
Nothing can be heard,
Even then and there,
For me everything
Is my faith in my God,
The Omnipotent.
He is always there.
The dark nights fade away
As my God says,
MAY THERE BE DAWN.

So Be It

MIRACLES OF WAITING FOR DAWN

Darkness creeps through,
Covering the embers of light
As nightfall approaches.
I stay awake and watch
The skies above for signs of light.
I hold my hands up
And bow my head down
As I recite my nightly prayers.
Oh my God,
Show me the path.
Guide me through life
As I walk alone on this path of life.
Oh my God,
How do I walk forward?
Where do I find the solutions
I seek to move on with life?
Oh my God,
Help me through my obstacles as I look
For the removal of all my obstacles.
Oh my God,
As darkness covers my path,
My destination,

And my journey,
I ask, seek, and knock
Upon Your door
For You to help me not lose faith,
Not lose hope,
And not lose belief
In my God,
My God's ways,
And my God's decisions for me.
I know
My God is the Merciful,
My God is the Healer,
My God is the Provider,
And my God is always there.
So, I, Your creation,
Shall let all my troubles pass over
For I know all my prayers
Shall find their answers.
Darkness will dissolve
After I,
With complete faith, belief, and hope,
Recite the prayer,
MIRACLES OF WAITING FOR DAWN.

So Be It

MIRACULOUS AMBER GLOW OF DAWN

Oh my God,
The Giver,
The Taker,
The Creator of me
And all that is above
And beyond,
I stay awake all night
In fear of
The known and unknown hurdles.
I remain in fear
Of the failures of life
And the unaccomplished tasks.
I am burdened
With financial, physical,
And emotional turmoil
That curl around me.
My God,
One thing I have
In my life
At all times,
Even during my struggles,
And the days

I thrive with success,
Is my faith.
I never lost faith.
I never lost hope.
I never gave up
On my God,
My Creator.
I told all
It is for my good,
You chose to give me pain.
It is for my good,
You made me suffer.
It is for my good,
I was surrounded
With only hurdles.
Yet today,
As I walk in the dark night
On a lonely path,
I ask You,
My Lord,
My Creator,
Please let me be successful.
Let me be
Financially stable.

Let me have love.
Let me have a life
Where my path is not
Filled with thorns,
Where my path is not
Blocked off with hurdles,
And where I too can have
Freedom to choose a life
With peace, joy, and harmony.
Like all Your creation,
I too am Your beloved creation,
Who never left
Your path.
In pain or in difficulties
Throughout life,
You my Lord
Have always been
There for me.
My love for You
And Your love for me
Has created a bond
Eternally tied with
Faith, hope, and belief
In my one God

And Your grace, mercy,
And forgiveness.
Your love and Your timing
Will come
As it is my time to be
Free from all obstacles.
As my prayers reach
Your door,
I ask, I seek, and I knock
All throughout
The dark night.
With complete faith,
I know my God,
You will answer my prayers.
As You tested my faith,
My hope,
And my belief,
Now finally,
After the darkest time,
My prayer calls are answered.
Like a miraculous call,
I witness the
MIRACULOUS AMBER GLOW OF DAWN.

So Be It

MIRACULOUS RADIATOR OF DAWN

My God, my Creator,
Up in Heaven You live,
Where there is only
Peace, love, and serenity.
Yet on Earth, we are thrust
Into fearsome lonely places,
And are asked to carry
Courage with us.
We face financial difficulties,
And are asked
To seek a job or ask for help.
We knock upon wrong doors,
And are asked to keep knocking
For the right door.
Tonight, I,
Your lost and stranded creation,
Recite my prayers
As I ask, seek, and knock
On Your door of mercy.
I am blessed as I have courage.
I am blessed as I am able to
Ask, seek, and knock for help.

As the road of life
Keeps bending and curving
At all corners,
May I, Your devoted creation,
Be blessed with Your guidance.
When I am searching for a way,
And when I need to make a decision,
May I find a solution.
May I knock upon the right door
As I knock for opportunities
To land behind one of the doors.
My God, my Creator,
As the nights seem longer,
And daylight feels shorter,
May I have Your blessings with me
Through dawn to dusk till dawn.
May my prayers reach Your door,
And may my prayers
Keep me protected
Throughout my journey on Earth.
I ask You tonight
To protect me and all of Your creation
Who are Your blessed children.
We, my God, ask, seek, and knock

Through our prayers
Only on Your doors.
I pray my God,
Let the dark night fade away,
And allow Your biggest glowing star,
Your brightest and blessed Sun to appear.
May the messages
Of the Omnipotent spread
Through the glowing rays of the Sun.
Where there are obstacles,
There are ways.
Where a creation seeks,
The answers are found.
It is then,
The darkness dissolves
And all witness the miraculous protection
For all of God's creation.
With love and blessings,
Heating the Earth,
The one and only,
With a smile from the Heavenly skies
Is the
MIRACULOUS RADIATOR OF DAWN.

So Be It

NEVER FEAR DARKNESS OR DAWN

Oh my God,
I, Your creation,
Am scared.
I am terrified
And am afraid
I have gotten lost.
All around me
I find only darkness.
I feel like
The cold shivering
Water of life
Is drowning me.
I find
All around me
Only obstacles
As I try to find
My way
Out of this
Horrific path of life.
I have
No one.
I have

Nothing.
I have
No direction,
So, I take a break
And pray.
With hands
Held up
High above
My head,
Bent down
On my knees,
I pray
Only to You,
My God,
My Creator,
To give me
Strength,
To give me
Courage,
To give me
Wisdom
To
NEVER FEAR DARKNESS OR DAWN.

So Be It

OBSTACLE-FREE BRIDGE AT DAWN

My God,
The Omnipotent,
Place me on
The obstacle-free bridge,
Where the footprints
Are made out of
Stress-free,
Worry-free,
And
Crisis-free
Stepping stones.
The footprints
Are imprinted with
Difficulty-free,
Physical-pain-free,
And
Emotional-pain-free
Wishes.
The pure
And innocent
Prayers
Of the pure

And innocent souls
Are answered.
The mind,
The body,
And the soul's
Obstacles are lifted
As the humans
Raise their pure hands,
In prayers
From the darkest night
Through the first sight of light.
We the humans
Pray with the pure mind.
Oh my God,
The Omnipotent,
With grace,
Mercy,
And blessings,
Lift all my obstacles
Through this blessed prayer
As I stand on the
Blessed
OBSTACLE-FREE BRIDGE AT DAWN.

So Be It

OPEN OUR EYES AT DAWN

Oh my God, my Creator,
Darkness evolves all around
As nightfall reaches
Your creation.
We walk
Through the darkness
With the taught lessons
Of our lives.
We try to get the direction
To the path
Where light evolves,
Where truth flows,
And where sweet water
Of immortal life is found.
We, Your creation,
Try to see through
The words of the others.
We follow the ones
Ahead of us
As we try to not get
Off the path all walk on.
We fear the darkness,

The loneliness,
And the wrong path,
So we stay behind the others
Who have walked
Ahead of us.
Yet as darkness falls
And the others we follow
Have gone lost,
We find ourselves
Lost and stranded
All over again.
I begin to pray
As I know
When and where
Everything is lost,
And nothing is found,
You, my God, my Creator,
Have never left.
You have sent
Your messages to
Not walk in the dark
But to
OPEN OUR EYES AT DAWN.

So Be It

PEACE BY DAWN

Oh my God, my Creator,
The Alpha, the Omega,
Tonight, I pray
For all Your creation
From all different faiths,
From all different cultures,
And from all different races
To love, respect, and honor
One another
As the one creation
Of the one Creator.
As everyone tries to weed out
The bad from the good,
And tries to protect oneself
From becoming
The dark night's prey,
May we not become
The divider, the unjust,
Or the dreadful one all fear.
Oh my God,
Let us the creation know
We are all the creation

Of the one Creator.
Tonight,
As everyone is divided,
As everyone is frightened,
And as everyone becomes the judge,
May we remember You,
My God,
The Creator of all creation,
Are the one and only Judge.
May we,
With complete faith and belief
In the complete truth
Of Your love for us,
And our love for You,
Love all Your creation equally.
By the end
Of the dark night,
We shall all unite and welcome
For one another,
With one another,
For the one God,
The Omnipotent,
PEACE BY DAWN.

So Be It

POURING LIGHT OF DAWN

As the Sun sets
And the land falls into darkness,
I, Your devotee,
Never fear,
Never lose hope,
And never get lost within the darkness
As I have You.
I have Your commandments.
I have Your chosen ways.
I have my faith, my will,
And my breath
To never get lost
Within the darkness.
I will hold on to my prayers
To guide me
Out of darkness into light,
As You, my God, my Creator,
Bless Your creation
With the first miracle of the day,
The
POURING LIGHT OF DAWN.

So Be It

PRAYER REQUEST AT DAWN

Oh my God, my Creator,
Tonight,
As everything turns dark,
Nothing can be visibly seen.
Nothing can be heard.
I, Your lost and stranded creation,
Pour my tears
In fear
And with pain
As I am overburdened
With grief.
For when and where
I have nothing,
I know I have You.
So, I, Your beloved creation,
Raise my hands
In prayer
Only to You.
I have come and
Landed at Your doors.
My God, my Creator,
Where do I leave

My waterfall
Of pouring tears?
My praying hands
Muffle my crying sounds,
So, they do not
Rip the silence
And be a bother to anyone
Walking upon
The dark night's path.
Oh my God,
I ask,
I knock,
And I seek
Your assistance through
The obstacles of my life
As I am swaying,
Dizzy with the hurdles
Crushing upon me.
I know You,
My God,
Hear my thoughts.
You see the pouring tears,
I hide from the world.
You know

My pure needs
And my innocent desires
For You are my Creator,
And I am Your creation.
So tonight,
With all my hope,
My faith,
And my belief,
I pray to You
For myself
From my innocent heart.
You, my God, know
I am the needy,
And I am the destitute
Who has no one
To provide for me
The answers
To my innocent prayers.
I believe those who have
No one,
No place,
Or no hope
Have You.
My God,

The Omnipotent,
The Omnipresent,
The Omniscient,
The Creator
Of all that is
And all that is not,
I pray to only You.
I knock upon only Your doors.
I ask for only You.
I seek only Your attention
As I send You
All my innocent wishes.
As I walk through
The dark night's scary path
Toward the first sign of light,
With complete hope,
Complete faith,
And complete belief that
You, my God,
Will answer my prayers,
I recite and send You,
My
PRAYER REQUEST AT DAWN.

So Be It

PROCLAMATION OF DAWN

As the longest night approaches,
I kneel
On my painful knees
And pray to You,
My God, my Creator,
To hold my hand.
Oh my God,
Support me from falling.
Oh my God,
Help me as I tonight
Learn to let go.
May I
Through this blessed prayer,
Let go of my fears.
Why should I fear
When You, my God,
Are always here?
I let go of my sorrows
As where there is suffering
And pain,
You, my God,
For the love of Your creation,

Always appear,
Gifting all laughter, joy, and harmony.
I let go of my stress,
As I see You have sent me
The past to learn from,
The present as a gift,
And the future,
Not to stress tonight and lose
What I have in my hands,
The gift of today.
My God shares the future
With us as we plan
And walk to it.
My God,
Be my guide as I travel
From today to tomorrow.
Oh my God,
As the night becomes darker
And the never-ending troubles
Become even brighter
In the fearful dark night,
I let go of my anger.
I know
I can only think and pray

When I am calm.
I do not want You to be angry
With me,
So I follow Your footsteps
And only walk
On the path of letting go.
My God, my Creator,
I wipe my tears with my hands
As I pray to You.
I shall let go of my tears
And allow them to fall freely,
So I can see what is ahead of me
And not miss out on
My blessings from You.
Oh my God,
Tonight,
I pray and recite to You.
I shall let go of
All past negative attributes.
I know as I let go,
I have changed my travel itinerary
And am on the bridge of personal growth.
I shall always
Let You be the Navigator of my life.

I shall travel upon
The path You have blessed,
Not the path
That was created through
Mistakes,
Attachments,
Arguments,
Dishonesty,
Pain,
And regrets.
For where You are my Lord,
There is only
The light of knowledge.
I shall on this dark,
And longest night,
Walk toward Your brightest star
Waiting to appear at dawn,
As I learn to let go
And free myself from
All negative attributes of life,
As I accept and recite
My
PROCLAMATION OF DAWN.

So Be It

PROTECTION FROM DUSK THROUGH DAWN

My God,

The Omnipotent,

I stand under the night's skies with

Pouring rain.

Lightning strikes

And thunder roars.

As I raise my hands,

I know there is no one,

There is no help,

And there is no safety

Within the embrace of loneliness,

Embrace of fear,

And embrace of worry.

Yet there is

Only

One

Who always arrives

And stands by me,

Holds my hands

And reassures me,

Everything will be

Just all right.

When tears pour,
Anger strikes,
And harsh words roar,
It is then and forever,
My one friend still smiles,
Still says it is okay,
And still says never fear for I am here.
The disbelievers ask,
Who is this invisible friend
Whom no one can see,
No one can hear,
And no one can feel?
I say to all,
It is my faith
That allows me to see Him,
To hear Him,
And to feel Him.
You all call Him
The Omnipotent.
From Him
And only Him,
I seek
PROTECTION FROM DUSK THROUGH DAWN.

So Be It

RAINY FOGGY DAWN

Oh my God,
The Creator of the universe
And all on,
Above,
And beyond,
I pray to You
As I walk
From dusk
Through dawn.
Your skies are roaring
As they pour down upon
Your creations.
All the birds are flying
As they search
For a safe home.
Oh my God,
I pray for all
The birds,
The stray animals,
And the humans
To be safe and secure
Through the storms of life.

As nightfall covers all
In the dark,
I pray for all to be safe
Through the dark night's
Cold, frigid, and wet paths
Till dawn.
I know
My God, my Creator,
The Omnipotent,
The Omnipresent,
The Omniscient,
Will cover all His creations
Within His embrace
To be safe,
To be secure,
And to not be
In any emotional
Or physical pain
As He pours
Rainfall down upon Earth
To clean
And wash away
All the troubles
Facing His creations.

So tonight,
As I wait for the Sun
To break through
Within a foggy
And rainy night,
I pray with all my heart
To my Creator,
The Omnipotent,
The Omnipresent,
The Omniscient,
To answer and accept
My prayers.
I know
My God, my Creator,
Is watching over
All His creations.
He will answer
And bless all today
As we are touched
By the blessed Heavenly rain
When we walk
Out of a dark night to a
RAINY FOGGY DAWN.

So Be It

REMOVE ALL FINANCIAL BURDENS BY DAWN

As darkness falls,
Everything becomes invisible.
We, Your creation,
Oh my God,
Close our eyes and pray
The financial burdens
We, Your creation, face
Shall disappear.
Oh my God,
My Creator,
Even the invisibility fog
Does not remove
The financial burdens.
Closing the eyes and hoping
For a better tomorrow
Does not work
As this world only exists
Through finances.
Minimum food
On plates,
Decent clothing
To cover shame,

And a shelter to protect us
From the outside world,
We do not have as we all fall prey
To finances.
So tonight,
With our minds, our bodies, and our souls,
We, the creation,
Recite this prayer
To You,
The one and only Creator,
The Omnipotent
The Omnipresent,
The Omniscient.
Even when and even where
We have no one,
We all believe with complete faith,
Complete belief,
And complete hope,
We have You.
With this faith, belief, and hope,
We pray
May You, our Creator,
REMOVE ALL FINANCIAL BURDENS BY DAWN.

So Be It

REMOVE ALL RACISM BY DAWN

My God, my Creator,
As I walk on
The cold freezing paths tonight,
I see a black child cry,
I see a brown child cry,
And I see a white child cry
As they walk together,
Yet separated by their parents
Who are infected
By race, color, and religion.
They teach themselves
And others
Discrimination
As they are infected
Through this impure poison.
They spread this germ
Near and far.
My God,
My heart holds safe
All the children of God,
In the one house
Of my inner temple.

As I cry for all the discriminated,
All the affected,
And all the divided children
Of my God,
The Omnipotent,
I ask You
Who created all
With Your blessed hands
To protect, save, and hold
These children
In the one house of Earth.
I, Your beloved creation,
Pray this prayer
Sent to You
From my inner temple
At the darkest hour of the night
On Earth.
Please my God,
With the miraculous command
Of Your blessings,
For the love
For all Your creation,
REMOVE ALL RACISM BY DAWN.

So Be It

REVERE DAWN'S BLESSED PRAYERS

Ocean waters glitter
Under the Sun's pouring rays.
Mountain breeze
Refreshes the Earth.
Drizzling rain
Cleans the grounds.
Oh my God, my Creator,
How blessed are
The wonders of
Your universe.
Oh my God, my Creator,
You have blessed us
With fruits,
With vegetables,
With grains
To satisfy our hunger,
And water to quench
Our thirst.
Oh my God, my Creator,
How blessed
Are we the creation,
As our Creator

Never left us.
Forever,
You, my God, my Creator,
Walk along
Your creation
As You never left us.
Yet I pray we,
The lost,
The stranded,
And the confused
Never leave You
And never get off
Your path
Or
Get disconnected
From You.
I will eternally
Be connected to You
Through
My faith,
My hope,
And my belief
As I
Worship only

You.
So tonight as
Darkness approaches,
I know
With all my faith,
Tonight's guiding lights
You have lit
Across the skies
Will take me
To the biggest star.
As dawn breaks open,
I worship only You.
For You,
I, Your devotee,
Recite my morning prayers
So we never
Get disconnected,
As I,
With all
My mind,
My body,
And my soul,
REVERE DAWN'S BLESSED PRAYERS.

So Be It

SHOWER YOUR BLESSINGS AT DAWN

Oh my God,
The Omnipotent,
Tonight, I pray for all my sins,
For all my wrongs,
To be forgiven
Through my repentance,
Redemption,
And awakening.
Oh my God,
Let there be forgiveness,
Let there be peace,
And let there be love
Within my soul.
Let my love
For You, my God,
Be my strength,
My guidance,
My path to the house of
The Omnipotent,
The Omnipresent,
The Omniscient.
As I pray

With my head bowed down,
And hands raised up only to You,
My God, my Creator,
May You
Through this blessed prayer,
Remove all my hurdles,
All my obstacles,
And all my physical and emotional pain.
I know a creation's prayer,
Never goes unheard
By the Omnipotent.
I, Your creation,
With complete faith,
Complete belief,
And complete hope,
Send out all my prayer requests
Through knocking,
Asking, and seeking for
My prayers to be answered.
May You, my God,
The Omnipotent,
With love,
SHOWER YOUR BLESSINGS AT DAWN.

So Be It

SPARKLING ARRAYS OF DAWN

Sparkling arrays
Of the sunset
Across the skies
Mesmerize the Earth.
Oh my God,
On this evening,
Reality paints a picture
As everything begins
To be covered
By darkness.
Oh my God,
I kneel and pray
For the darkness
To not engulf me
Onto the wrong path,
Amongst the wrong crowd,
Or embraced within sinful acts.
Oh my God,
I raise my hands,
Not in the deadly sins,
But I raise my hands
In prayer

To You
For I know
All the temptations,
All the greed,
And all the failures
Of self-control
Are through the touch
Of the darkness.
Oh my God.
I pray with all my faith,
All my hope,
And all my love
To not fall prey
To the darkness
But be touched by You,
Be blessed by You,
And be forgiven by You.
I am blessed
To wait out
The darkness
And be touched
By Your blessed
SPARKLING ARRAYS OF DAWN.

So Be It

STRENGTH FROM DUSK TO DAWN

I pray to
My God,
The Omnipotent,
To keep me protected,
To keep me safe,
To keep me healthy,
To keep me wealthy,
To keep me happy,
And to keep me wise.
I pray to
My God,
The Omnipotent,
May I find solace within my faith
And have my belief,
My hope,
And my prayers
Guide me through
The journey of life.
May prayers be
My
STRENGTH FROM DUSK TO DAWN.

So Be It

SUN WILL RISE AT DAWN

When the day ends
And shadows of dusk
Fall on Earth,
All the tired
And restless creation
Try to return home.
Oh my God, my Creator,
Keep us Your creation safe.
Let us have
Warm food
On our plates.
Oh my God, my Creator,
May we have
A place to call
Our home,
Where we are
Protected
From all intruders,
And all unwanted predators.
The walls will protect us
From the cold,
The rain,

And the storms of life.
Oh my God, my Creator,
Let all the obstacles be removed,
As I walk on this lonely
Obstacle-filled path at dusk.
I know I must
Walk through
The dark night's hurdles
With nothing but
My faith,
My belief,
And my hope.
I know
My God, my Creator,
I have a
Direct connection with You
Through my
Innocent call
Of prayers.
I believe and know
My prayers
Will reach
My God, my Creator.
All night,

As I light
My lanterns of hope,
I know
My God, my Creator,
Will light
His biggest
Candle of hope
For me
And all who
Believe in prayers,
Who pray,
Who hope,
And who never give up.
All will find
After the darkest night,
My God, my Creator,
The Omnipresent,
The Omnipotent,
The Omniscient,
Will accept our prayers
As after the storm,
The
SUN WILL RISE AT DAWN.

So Be It

TEMPTED FROM DAWN

Grave night's darkness
Spreads
Around
Covering the dark sins
Of the night.
Oh my God,
I, Your creation,
Must walk
Through this dark
Grave path
As I have only
One way to go.
Yet as I walk
Through
The path of sin,
I repeat,
I shall not sin.
As I walk through
The path of lust,
I repeat,
I shall have no lust.
As I walk through

The path of envy,
I repeat,
I shall not envy.
As I walk through
The path of gluttony,
I repeat,
Gluttony touches me not.
As I walk through
The path of greed,
I repeat,
I am not greedy.
Throughout
The journey of my life,
I repeat,
I have within my
Carry-on luggage,
The glad tidings
Of my Creator,
My God,
The Omnipotent,
As I the creation
Am never
TEMPTED FROM DAWN.

So Be It

THROUGH BREAKING DAWN

Oh my God,

The Omnipotent,

Tonight as I walk

Through the obstacles of life,

I ask my faith

To be my guide.

I ask hope

To be my path.

I ask mercy

To forgive my mistakes.

I ask blessings

To be my friend.

I ask fear

To remove its company.

As I ask, seek, and knock on all doors

Through the dark and lonely night,

I pray

My God,

The Omnipotent,

Accepts my prayers as He answers

THROUGH BREAKING DAWN.

So Be It

THROUGH DARKNESS THROUGH DAWN

Winds ripple through
Churning the ocean,
Causing
Twisters on Earth
And thunderstorms
In the skies
As I, Your creation,
Am flying alone
Like a lonely bird.
I have no family.
I have no friends.
I have no support,
Yet I
Hold on to You,
My God.
I hold on to
My faith in You
As I
Stand upon
The ark
Of my faith
Within the churning ocean.

I stand

Shielded under

My faith

As a tornado

Tears across

The Earth.

I stand

Protected within

The cave of my faith

While a thunderstorm

Rips through

The skies.

Oh my God,

My Creator,

I,

The traveler of life,

Will never fall prey

To the obstacles

Of life

As

I have my

Ever-glowing faith

THROUGH DARKNESS THROUGH DAWN.

So Be It

THROUGH THE FIRST BREAK OF DAWN

I pray to my Lord,
My God, my Creator.
I awaken at dawn as darkness fades
And daylight greets and reminds me,
I have so much work,
So many obligations,
I must take care of.
I cannot stay in bed.
So, I take a deep breath
And I call upon You first,
Oh my God, my Creator.
All can be lost,
All can be gone,
And all can be forgotten,
Yet not You,
My God, my Creator.
Even when no one is here
For me,
Or no helping hands
Will support me,
I hold on to my faith
With all my hope,

And my strength in my belief.
Even when I do not see You,
And I do not hear You,
I do feel You
Through the miracle of a prayer
Which is my ark,
My strength,
And my guidance for
How to walk and work
Through my day.
With this blessed prayer
I can even walk through
The dark streets of the night,
As my prayers
Become
My candles of hope,
Which I hold on to
Throughout the night.
Oh my God, my Creator,
I hold on to my blessed prayers
As my life's floating bridge
From the first sign of darkness
THROUGH THE FIRST BREAK OF DAWN.

So Be It

THROUGH THE RAYS OF DAWN

Oh my God,
The dark night's lonely corridors
Can hear my heartbeats.
At the slightest creeks of a door,
My heartbeats rise.
At the first loud screams of a person,
My heartbeats rise.
Frightened, scared,
And petrified
By the intruders and the invaders,
My heartbeats rise.
The unknown and unseen enemies
Loom around
With so much power,
So much pride,
And so much confidence.
They can wash out, wipe out,
And bring down
A frightened lonely person.
They can stand over,
They can stomp over,
And they can bully over

A frightened lonely person
Who in fear,
Does not talk back,
Does not shout back,
And does not stand up
For own self,
Own dignity
Or own pride.
Yet tonight,
I, Your frightened creation,
My God, my Creator,
Ask, knock, and seek for You to
Give me strength,
Give me dignity,
Give me a voice
To say no to the wrong
And stand up on my feet
By holding on to
Your hand,
My God, my Creator.
I pray to You
To bless me and remove my fears,
THROUGH THE RAYS OF DAWN.

So Be It

TROUBLES BE OVER BY DAWN

My God,
The Omnipotent,
Through this blessed prayer,
Give us,
Your creation,
Your blessed humans,
Who ask,
Knock,
And seek
Only You,
The divine guidance,
The divine protection,
The divine intervention,
The divine grace,
The divine forgiveness,
And the divine mercy.
Today,
As we walk
Through the
Lonely,
Frightful,
And dangerous

Paths,
We
Never forget
To pray,
Nor do we
Go astray
Through all
The temptations of life.
To be safe,
To be secure,
And to be happy,
We pray to You
My God, my Creator,
As You are
Our Creator,
The Omnipotent.
Through this prayer
May I,
Your creation,
Be protected
And may all
My
TROUBLES BE OVER BY DAWN.

So Be It

TRUE GLORY OF DAWN

Oh my God, my Creator,
As the Sun sets below the horizon,
I know the Earth I stand upon
Has rotated away.
May I, Your devoted creation,
Never forget You,
And never in the dark,
Get off Your path.
Far away from the Sun, I may be,
Or far away from
Where You are physically,
Yet I will always be there with You,
Through my faith, my belief,
And my love for You,
My God, my Creator.
Tonight, as darkness
Appears around me,
I pray may I not be too sleepy,
Not be too tired,
Not be too fatigued,
And not be too depressed
Through all the hurdles of life.

May I have the energy and the alertness.
May I be happy for what I have
And not overburdened
And frightful for what I do not have.
My God, I ask You
To grant me joy.
Make me energetic
And make me fearless.
So, during the night
When the Sun is not there,
Give me energy
And make things brighter,
So I can still stay awake and pray.
This earthly vehicle
At times because of tiredness,
Does not align
With the spiritual path,
Where I want to do
So much more,
Yet can only achieve so much.
Hear my pleas, my God,
And allow me to
Do what You want me to do,
Not what

This world wants me to do.
Grant me courage.
Give me the strength
And hold on to me,
So I, Your creation,
Can achieve all that I must
As per Your commands.
Give me the knowledge
To perform my job on Earth
As per Your wishes.
Accept my pleas, my God,
As I watch the Earth rotate again
Beneath my feet,
And I witness the first glimpse of light.
I know my prayers
Will be answered,
As I have stayed awake,
Praying from
The first sight of dusk through
The first sight of dawn.
I witness in front of me,
The
TRUE GLORY OF DAWN.

So Be It

TWIN FLAME AT DAWN

Oh my God,
I, Your creation,
Am single and happy,
Yet Your other creation
Question my way.
They ask questions
About my character
For being single,
For being pious,
For not falling to temptations
Of the dark night's sinful ways.
I pray to You, my God
For protection.
May I not fall prey to temptation.
May I not go astray in
The dark night's lost paths.
May my mind, my body,
And my soul
Always be protected.
Oh my God,
May the tempting words,
And the sweet musical notes

Not drift my mind, my body,
And my soul
Through the dark night's temptations.
May I be strong.
May I be devoted.
May I know the temptations
Of the dark nights are
Just that, temptations,
Which fade at the
First sight of light.
May
My mind,
My body,
And
My soul
Wait for
The purest blessings
And know
The Lord shall provide.
The Lord shall send.
The Lord will unite
With me my
TWIN FLAME AT DAWN.

So Be It

UNITED AT DAWN

Oh my God,
The Omnipotent,
Tonight,
I pray for
Your creation
Across Your Earth
To love one another,
To respect one another,
To honor one another,
And to understand one another
As we are all Your creation.
You created all colors,
All races,
And all religions.
You created good.
You created bad.
You created the angels,
The humans,
And the animals,
All with Your blessed hands.
Today,
I, Your creation,

Ask,
Seek,
And knock
Upon
Your door
To make all of us,
Your creation,
Love,
Honor,
And respect one another.
My God, my Creator,
Let all the
Anger,
The hate,
And the divisions
Be erased with
Love,
Kindness,
Mercy,
And forgiveness
As You, my God,
Are the eternal love,
Eternal mercy,
And eternal forgiveness.

Oh my God,
As the night
Grows darker,
And Your creation
Get lost
On their own path,
I pray to You,
May all
The lost and stranded
Find their ways back to You.
May we all realize
There is but
One Creator
As we are all
Your one creation.
With this knowledge,
I pray may we,
Your one creation,
Walk out
Of the divided dark night
To glorify the truth
And be
UNITED AT DAWN.

So Be It

VEIL OF DARKNESS THROUGH DAWN

Forgiveness,
Oh my God,
Is Your mercy,
Not my fear.
My God,
Where there is
Fear,
Where there is
Doubt,
And where there is
Self-examination,
The answer,
My God,
Is never found.
The answer
Comes as Your mercy.
For all humans,
There is
One path,
One truth,
And one direction,
The one God,

The one Creator,
The All-Knowing,
The All-Forgiving,
Who is mine
And
Everyone's Creator.
My God,
The Omnipotent,
Forgives
Even when
We do not forgive
As we are all
Walking within
The darkness of doubt.
My God
Is
The Merciful
And the Forgiver
As He
Removes
Through forgiveness
The
VEIL OF DARKNESS THROUGH DAWN.

So Be It

VENERATION AT DAWN

As the day becomes dark,
I begin to pray.
The dark night's
Array of obstacles
Freezes my mind,
My body,
And my soul.
The fear bestowed
By all the hurdles
Terrifies my inner being
And converts me
Into nothing
But a heavy statue
Made out of stones.
Yet my Lord,
My body still feels.
My eyes still pour out tears.
The pain and hurt
Inflicted upon my entire being
Break me apart,
Even though
I have converted myself

Into stone.
Oh my God,
I still suffer through
The financial burdens.
I still suffer through
The physical pain.
I still feel the emotional pain.
Tonight,
As I let my tears fall,
I try to survive
The dark
And dangerous night.
Nothing is found here.
Nothing is achieved.
Nothing is available,
Yet here within all the hurdles,
All the difficulties
Life could bestow upon me,
I lift myself up.
I stand on my feet.
I carry on with life.
Holding on to
Faith,
Hope,

Strength,
Dignity,
And courage,
I take one step at a time
Toward my goals.
Yet first,
My God, my Creator,
I pause and mourn
The creation of Yours
I have lost,
As You gifted
Your creation
Temporarily to me.
I know all lives
Belong to You
And they must
Return to You
As they love You.
I love You more than
All that is on and above Earth.
Yet my God,
It hurts.
It tears me apart
As I am weak.

I am alone and I feel lost.
I pray to You, my God,
To make me strong.
Make me stable.
Give me strength
To move on and walk
Through this life
With complete faith and honor.
I know nothing is lost
As I do not see or hear You,
Yet I know
You, my God, are there.
So, I know those whom
I have lost,
I cannot see but
They are blessed
For they are with You
As they belonged to You
And have returned to You.
Tonight, I pray to You,
My God, my Creator,
To hear my prayers
And lessen my burdens.
May I be blessed with

Your grace,
Your mercy,
And Your love,
So, I too can walk again
And hold my head up
Not in fear,
Not in pain,
Not in terror,
But with dignity.
Oh my God,
Accept my prayers
And let this night
Fade away
At the first sight
Of the Sun's glare.
I know my God hears.
I know my God answers.
I know my God accepts
All prayers calls,
As You answer
All on Earth
Through
VENERATION AT DAWN.

So Be It

VICTORY OF DAWN

Oh my God,
My Creator,
The cold shivering nights,
And the slippery paths
Covered with fallen leaves,
Hiding dangerous obstructions
All around,
That my eyes,
My senses,
And my pure and clean soul,
Try to avoid,
Are coming to an end.
I know after winter,
You,
My God,
My Creator,
Reassure
And bless Your creation
With spring.
The glowing illumination
Of the full Moon
Guides all creation

Through the dark
And cold nights.
My God,
My Creator,
Reassures all creation
After all difficulties,
All darkness,
All sorrows,
And all sadness,
Victory always
Belongs to good
Over evil.
As darkness evaporates
At the first sprinkle
Of the colorful light pouring
Through the
Night's skies,
I see
My God's blessings,
To all His creation,
Through
The
VICTORY OF DAWN.

So Be It

VOW OF DAWN

Oh my God, my Creator
I walk through the darkest
And scariest streets
As I feel lost,
As I feel lonely,
And as I feel unloved.
Yet as I watch
The twinkling stars
Of the night's skies,
And the glorious Moon
Shining on the streets,
I know
My God, my Creator,
Is there.
So tonight,
I will not complain.
I will not ask.
I will not seek.
I will not knock.
I will tell You,
My God, my Creator,
I am here

To praise You.
I am here to remember You.
I am here
And will always pray only
To You,
For I have my faith
And my glowing hope
With me.
Even when no one prays,
No one remembers,
No one raises their hands in prayer,
And no one bows their heads
In prayer,
I will always be there.
I have my steadfast faith,
And my immortal hope
Breathing within my chest.
As long as I breathe,
This devotee
Will love You,
My God,
The Omnipotent,
For not what
I have received,

Or what I have lost,
But because
My mind,
My body,
And my soul
Belong to You
As I am Your creation
And You
Are my Creator.
Oh my God,
This creation
Shall eternally
Remember,
My Creator's
Love,
Mercy,
Grace,
And
Forgiveness
As my first
Prayers of dawn,
As this is my
VOW OF DAWN.

So Be It

WISHED UPON THIS DAWN

Oh my God,
My Creator,
As the stars appeared
Upon the Heavenly skies,
I wished
From my mind,
Through my body,
And with all my inner soul.
I wished
For my inner prayers,
My inner wishes,
To be heard,
To be seen,
To be accepted,
By You,
My God,
My Creator.
As I wondered all night
Why even after
Wishing upon the stars
My prayers
Were not accepted

Or answered,
I saw
The biggest star
Came and knocked
Upon my windows.
As dawn broke open
After the dark night's struggles,
I saw
Not all the twinkling stars
But there in
The vast dawn skies
Was shining
The biggest
And the brightest star,
The Sun.
So, with the Sun
As my witness,
I pray to You,
My God,
My Creator,
To accept my wishes
I have
WISHED UPON THIS DAWN.

So Be It

YOUR FULL MOON BEFORE DAWN

My God, my Creator,
The Sun is setting,
Upon Your Earth.
The busy and dangerous streets
Are filled with sins,
As Your creation
Now have come out,
Not afraid
To do wrong onto others.
They fear not
Their own wrongs.
They fear not
The unfortunate events that
Their committed sins
And their committed crimes
Cause on the innocent.
Oh my God,
At this time,
I, Your creation,
Your true devotee,
Pray to You
For forgiveness.

I pray to You
For guidance.
I pray to You
For a path to be opened,
So that I,
Your creation,
Your devoted devotee,
Can find an escape
From the dark night's
Sinful crimes,
The unsafe roads,
And the risky people.
They care not
For themselves
Nor do they care
For all whom
They step upon.
Lift me miraculously,
My God, my Creator.
With Your mercy, blessings, and grace,
Take me
To a safe place
Which has been
Blessed by You

Through Your grace,
And Your mercy.
Tonight,
I, Your devotee,
Ask, knock, and seek
For protection from You,
My God, my Creator,
The Protector of all
Your creation.
I, Your devoted creation,
Raise my hands
Only to You.
Accept my prayer requests
As I have no one on Earth
But only You.
I find hope and faith
From Your celestial creation,
For as the Sun sets,
I see from the beyond,
You have sent a message that
All shall be all right
With
YOUR FULL MOON BEFORE DAWN.

So Be It

ABOUT THE AUTHOR

"Meet Ann Marie Ruby from Nashville, Tennessee. This is her story."

Ann Marie Ruby was born into a diplomatic family for which she had the privilege of traveling the world. This upbringing made the whole world her one family. She never saw a country as a foreign country yet as a neighbor who was there for her as she would be there for them. After all, isn't that what families do for one another?

Ann Marie became an author as she started to place her chosen words into the pages of her diaries. She knew she must collect all her thoughts and produce them into different diaries. Each diary became her different books.

Ann Marie's life goal is not to just write something but only what she believes in. So all her thoughts and words remained within the pages of her diaries until she realized it was time she must share them with you. Otherwise, she felt selfish and knew that was not her characteristic as she lives for everyone, not just for herself.

INTERNATIONAL #1 BESTSELLING AUTHOR:

Ann Marie became an international number-one bestselling author of twenty-nine books. Alongside being a full-time author. She loves to write articles on her website where she can have a better connection with all of you. Ann Marie, a dream psychic, became a blogger and a humanitarian only because she believes in you and herself as a complete, honest, and open family.

PERSONAL:

Ann Marie is an American who grew up in Brisbane, Australia. She has resided all across the United States and is currently living in Nashville, Tennessee. In her spare time when she is not writing books, she loves to meditate, pray, listen to music, cook, and write blog posts.

BESTSELLING:

Ann Marie's books have placed her on top 100 bestselling charts in various countries including the Netherlands, United States, United Kingdom, Canada, and Germany. In 2020, she became a household name as her books began to consistently rank #1 on multiple bestselling charts. *The Netherlands: Land Of My Dreams* and *Everblooming: Through The Twelve Provinces Of The Netherlands*, both became overnight number-one bestsellers in the United States.

In 2020, *The Netherlands: Land Of My Dreams* also became a bestseller in the Netherlands and Canada, consistently becoming #1 on various lists and one of the top selling books on Amazon NL. *Everblooming: Through The Twelve Provinces Of The Netherlands* became #37 on the Netherlands top 100 bestselling Amazon books chart which includes all books from all genres. Ann Marie's other books have also made various top 100 bestselling lists and received multiple accolades including *Eternal Truth: The Tunnel Of Light* which was named as one of eight thought-provoking books by women.

ROMANCE FICTION:

Ann Marie's *Kasteel Vrederic* series was written in a diary fashion. She has always kept a diary herself, so she thought her characters too could keep a diary. All of their diaries became individual books yet collectively, they are a part of a family, the Kasteel Vrederic family.

OTHER BOOKS:

All of Ann Marie's nonfiction and fiction books are available globally. You can take a look at the titles at the end of this book.

THE NETHERLANDS:

Ann Marie revealed why many of her books revolve around the Netherlands, sharing that as a dream psychic, she had seen the historical past of a country in her dreams and was later able to place a name to the country. This is described in detail in *Spiritual Lighthouse: The Dream Diaries Of Ann Marie Ruby* and *The Netherlands: Land Of My Dreams* where she also wrote about her plans to eventually move to the Netherlands.

Ann Marie has received letters on behalf of His Majesty King Willem-Alexander and Her Majesty Queen Máxima of the Netherlands after they received her books *The Netherlands: Land Of My Dreams* and *Everblooming: Through The Twelve Provinces Of The Netherlands*. Additionally, Ann Marie has received letters on behalf of His Excellency Mark Rutte, the Prime Minister of the Netherlands for her books.

WRITING:

Ann Marie also is acclaimed globally as one of the top voices in the spiritual space, however, she is recognized for her writing abilities published across many genres namely spirituality, lifestyle, inspirational quotations, poetry, fiction, romance, history, travel, social awareness, and more. Her writing style is hailed by critics and readers alike as making readers feel as though they have made a friend.

FOLLOW THE AUTHOR:

Now as you have found her book, why don't you and Ann Marie become friends? Join her and become a part of her global family. Ann Marie shall always give you books which you will read and then find yourself as a part of her book family.

For more information about Ann Marie Ruby, any one of her books, or to read her blog posts and articles, subscribe to her website, www.annmarieruby.com.

Follow Ann Marie Ruby on Twitter, Facebook, Instagram, Threads, and Pinterest:

@TheAnnMarieRuby

BOOKS BY THE AUTHOR

INSPIRATIONAL QUOTATIONS:

1. *Spiritual Travelers: Life's Journey From The Past To The Present For The Future*
2. *Spiritual Messages: From A Bottle*
3. *Spiritual Journey: Life's Eternal Blessings*
4. *Spiritual Inspirations: Sacred Words Of Wisdom*
5. *Spiritual Ark: The Enchanted Journey Of Timeless Quotations*

SPIRITUAL SONGS SERIES:

1. *Spiritual Songs: Letters From My Chest*
2. *Spiritual Songs II: Blessings From A Sacred Soul*
3. *Spiritual Songs III: The Rising Lotus*
4. *Spiritual Songs IV: Dusk Through Dawn*
5. *Spiritual Songs V: Dawn Through Dusk*

KASTEEL VREDERIC SERIES:

1. *Eternally Beloved: I Shall Never Let You Go*
2. *Evermore Beloved: I Shall Never Let You Go*
3. *Be My Destiny: Vows From The Beyond*
4. *Heart Beats Your Name: Vows From The Beyond*
5. *Entranced Beloved: I Shall Never Let You Go*
6. *Forbidden Daughter Of Kasteel Vrederic: Vows From The Beyond*
7. *The Immortality Serum: Vows From The Beyond*
8. *Woman In The Mirror: Vows From The Beyond*

Upcoming – *Bride Of The Immortal: Vows From The Beyond*

RELATED TO THE *KASTEEL VREDERIC* SERIES:

1. *Shattered Wings: Diary Of A Child Bride*

2. *The Bride, The Groom, And The Ghost*
3. *The Haunting Of MacNider Hospital*
4. *Enchanted Tales: A Kasteel Vrederic Storybook For Children*

Upcoming – *Brother Bear And The Four Investigators: A Kasteel Vrederic Storybook For Children*

NONFICTION:

1. *Spiritual Lighthouse: The Dream Diaries Of Ann Marie Ruby*
2. *The World Hate Crisis: Through The Eyes Of A Dream Psychic*
3. *Eternal Truth: The Tunnel Of Light*

TRAVEL:

1. *The Netherlands: Land Of My Dreams*
2. *Everblooming: Through The Twelve Provinces Of The Netherlands*

POETRY:

1. *Love Letters: The Timeless Treasure*
2. *Melodies Of Humanity: The Golden Keys*

www.ingramcontent.com/pod-product-compliance
Lightning Source LLC
LaVergne TN
LVHW011218080426
835509LV00005B/196
9798991741668